THE COLLECTED POEMS

OF JEAN TOOMER

THE COLLECTED

POEMS OF

Jean Toomer

EDITED BY ROBERT B. JONES

AND MARGERY TOOMER LATIMER

WITH AN INTRODUCTION AND TEXTUAL NOTES

BY ROBERT B. JONES

THE UNIVERSITY OF NORTH CAROLINA PRESS

CHAPEL HILL & LONDON

Library of Congress Cataloging-in-Publication Data

Toomer, Jean, 1894–1967.

  The collected poems of Jean Toomer.

  "A Publication history of the poetry of Jean
Toomer": p.

  I. Jones, Robert B. II. Latimer, Margery Toomer.
III. Title.

PS3539.0478A17   1988   811'.52   87-19203

ISBN 0-8078-1773-2

ISBN 0-8078-4209-5 (pbk.)

The paper in this book meets the guidelines for
permanence and durability of the Committee on
Production Guidelines for Book Longevity of the
Council on Library Resources.

92 91 90 89   5 4 3 2

The editors gratefully acknowledge
permission to reproduce thirty-three
unpublished poems from the Jean Toomer
Collection, Beinecke Rare Book and
Manuscript Library, Yale University.

CONTENTS

INTRODUCTION

I

Jean Toomer's popularity as a writer derives almost exclusively from his lyrical narrative, *Cane*. He shows himself there to be a poet, but few are aware of the extensive and impressive corpus of his other poems. His poetry canon may be classified into three categories: the individually published poems, the poems first published in *Cane*, and the mass of over one hundred unpublished poems.[1] To date, however, there has been no attempt to assemble a standard edition of Toomer's poetical works, nor has there been any comprehensive study of his poems.[2] Yet it is through the lens of his poetry that we are provided the most revealing commentaries on Toomer as artist and philosopher.

Toomer's poetry spans more than three decades and evolves in four distinct periods: the Aesthetic period (1919–August 1921), marked by Imagism, improvisation, and experimentation; the Ancestral Consciousness period (September 1921–23), characterized by forms of racial consciousness and Afro-American mysticism; the Objective Consciousness period (1924–39), defined by Gurdjieffian idealism and "being consciousness"; and the Christian Existential period (1940–55), derived from an espousal of Quaker religious philosophy. His poetry canon, then, constitutes a dramatization of consciousness, a veritable phenomenology of the spirit.

Toomer's career as a poet began long before the publication of *Cane*. Between 1919 and 1921 he experimented with several forms of poetry, including haiku, lyrical impressionism, and "sound poetry." The major influences on his artistic and philosophical development during this period were Orientalism, French and American Symbolism, and Imagism. Orientalism provided the basis for the idealist philosophy evident in all stages of Toomer's intellectual development. As he described it, "Buddhist philosophy, the Eastern teachings, occultism, theosophy . . . challenged and stimulated me. Despite my literary purpose, I was compelled to know something more about them. So for a long time I turned my back on literature and plunged into this kind of reading. I read far and wide, for more than eight months."[3] In a literary context, Orientalism was also the basis for his fascination with Symbolism and Imagism. Of the French Symbolists, his literary mentor was Charles Baudelaire, whose *Les Petits Poèmes en prose* inspired many of the poems written during this period and later provided models for the prose poems and lyrical sketches in *Cane*. To an even greater degree, he was impressed by the poetry and aesthetics of the Imagists. "Their insistence on fresh vision and on the perfect clean economical line was just what I had been looking for. I began feeling that I had in my hands the tools for my own creation."[4]

The best examples of the Imagist poetry from this period are "And Pass," "Storm Ending," "Her Lips Are Copper Wire," and "Five Vignettes." A sustained impressionistic portrait of twilight fading into darkness, "And Pass" images a picturesque sea setting in two brief movements, each introduced by "When." The poem concludes in a moment of visionary awareness, when the poet's imagination is suddenly arrested by the passing clouds, the fleeting and majestic "proud shadows." Concomitant with the poet's sense of exaltation comes a sense of his own loneliness and mortality, as "night envelops/empty seas/and fading dreamships."

Also richly impressionistic in design, "Storm Ending" unfolds as an implied comparison between two natural phenomena, thunder and flowers, although imagery remains the crucial vehicle of meaning:

> Thunder blossoms gorgeously above our heads,
> Great, hollow, bell-like flowers,
> Rumbling in the wind,
> Stretching clappers to strike our ears . .
> Full-lipped flowers
> Bitten by the sun
> Bleeding rain
> Dripping rain like golden honey—
> And the sweet earth flying from the thunder.

This scene captures the momentous return of sunshine and tranquility following a tempest, as the sound of thunder fades into the distance.

In "Her Lips Are Copper Wire," desire generated by a kiss is compared to electrical energy conducted between copper wires, here imaged as lips. The evocative and sensuous opening lines, addressed to the imaginary lover, well illustrate Pound's Doctrine of the Image.

whisper of yellow globes
gleaming on lamp-posts that sway
like bootleg licker drinkers in the fog

and let your breath be moist against me
like bright beads on yellow globes . . .

"Five Vignettes" is a series of imagistic sketches modeled after Japanese
haiku poetry. The first is a seascape portrait of "red-tiled ships" shim-
mering iridescently upon the water. The ships are "nervous" under the
threat of clouds eclipsing their watery reflections:

The red-tiled ships you see reflected,
Are nervous,
And afraid of clouds.

The second images a dynamic tension between stasis and motion:

There, on the clothes-line
Still as she pinned them,
Pieces now the wind may wear.

The third vignette images an old man of ninety, still living courageously,
"eating peaches" and unafraid of the "worms" that threaten his very
existence. The fourth is reminiscent of an Oriental proverb, especially in
its idea that suffering teaches wisdom; and the fifth images a Chinese
infant, as well as our common humanity:

In Y. Don's laundry
A Chinese baby fell
And cried as any other.

Vignettes four and five are as moral as they are imagistic, each in its own
way commenting on the universal human condition. As we shall see,
these message-oriented lyrics signal a subtle shift in Toomer's pre-*Cane*
aesthetic, which is more conspicuously apparent in the poems "Banking
Coal" and "Gum." The basis for this shift from an imitative toward an

affective theory of art is most clearly articulated in his 1921 review of Richard Aldington's essay on Imagism, "The Art of Poetry."[5]

Several of the poetic sketches recall the linguistic impressionism of Gertrude Stein's *Tender Buttons*, especially "Face" and the lyrical quartet "Air," "Earth," "Fire," and "Water." In *Tender Buttons*, Stein attempted to defamiliarize our automatic linguistic perceptions by creating a noun headnote without naming it, as she illustrates in "A Carafe, That Is a Blind Glass":

> A kind in glass and a cousin, a spectacle and
>   nothing strange
> A single hurt color and an arrangement in a system
>   to pointing
> All this and not ordinary, but unordered in not
>   resembling.
> The difference is spreading.[6]

This lyrical sketch is reminiscent of a riddle: "What is made of glass (and its 'cousin') but is different from a drinking glass in the way it spreads (bulbously) at the bottom?" The answer would be a carafe. Like Stein, Toomer attempted to register precise nuances of perception and name them with a unique word or phrase. Here he renders an image of the noun headnote "Face":

> Hair—
> silver-gray,
> like streams of stars,
> Brows—
> recurved canoes
> quivered by the ripples blown by pain,
> Her eyes—
> mists of tears
> condensing on the flesh below

Toomer's quartet ensemble also demonstrates how linguistic impressionism serves as a poetic medium for communicating both the uniqueness and universality of our common perceptions of the cosmic order, as in "Fire":

> Flickers, flames, burns.
> Burns into a thing—hence, depth, profundity
> "Hot after something,"
> Sparking, flowing, "in a fever"
> Always stewing smoking panting
> Flashy.

Yet another form of linguistic impressionism is revealed in "Sound Poem" (I), "Sound Poem" (II), and "Poem in C," all of which represent adaptations of French Symbolist aesthetics. The French Symbolists maintained that the purpose of language is to evoke a reality beyond the senses, rather than to state plainly or to inform. In their attempts to describe the *essence* of an object and not the object itself, they sought to produce the effects of music, thinking of images as having abstract values like musical notes and chords. Sounds and associations, then, perform the act of communication, while meaning is eclipsed, as in "Sound Poem" (I):

> Mon sa me el kirimoor,
> Ve dice kor, korrand ve deer,
> Leet vire or sand vite,
> Re sive tas tor;
> Tu tas tire or re sim bire,
> Rozan dire ras to por tantor,
> Dorozire, soron,
> Bas ber vind can sor, gosham,
> Mon sa me el, a som on oor.

Here Tomer uses sounds and words from several languages, such as French ("mon sa me" or "mon sommeil"; "vite"; "tas"; "bas"), Latin ("kor" and "soron"), Spanish ("me"; "el"; "dice"; "tu"; "por"), Japanese ("kirimoor"), and English to open poetic avenues to thought, in the tradition of Rimbaud, Baudelaire, and Laforgue. An exercise in formalism and a lesson in the mystical powers of language, this sound poem also employs "-or" end rhymes, "-ire" internal rhymes, repetition ("mon sa me el"), parallelism ("Leet vire or sand vite" and "Tu tas tire or re sim bire"), and linguistic cognates to create the illusion of meaning, while sounds guide us through the process of poetry.

II

In the months between September 1921 and December 1922, Toomer wrote the poems in *Cane* evocative of an empathetic union between the spirit of the artist and the spirit of Afro-American mysticism. Indeed, in describing formal design in *Cane*, which he termed "the spiritual entity behind the work," Toomer indicates that he viewed the book, at least retrospectively, as a mandala: "From the point of view of the spiritual entity behind the work, the curve really starts with 'Bona and Paul' (awakening), plunges into 'Kabnis,' emerges in 'Karintha,' etc., swings upward into 'Theater' and 'Box Seat,' and ends (pauses) in 'Harvest Song.' "[7] The mandala, a symbol of integration and transmutation of the self in Buddhist philosophy, is an arrangement of images from the unconscious forming a constellation. Usually a formalized, circular design containing or contained by a figure of five points of emphasis, each representing the chief objects of psychic interest for the maker, a mandala functions to unite the conscious intellectual perceptions of the creator with his unconscious psychic drives and intuitions. A mandala, then, is both an instrument of the self's awakening and a chart of its spiritual evolution. In accordance with Toomer's spiritual design, the poems that begin this mandalic cycle—"Reapers," "November Cotton Flower," "Cotton Song," "Song of the Sun," "Georgia Dusk," "Nullo," "Conversion," and "Portrait in Georgia"—represent celebrations of ancestral consciousness, whereas those that end the cycle—"Beehive," "Prayer," and "Harvest Song"—chronicle the poet's loss of empathetic union with Afro-American consciousness.

The poems which begin the cycle celebrate Afro-American culture and lament its disappearance. Written in iambic pentameter couplets, "Reapers" depicts black workers in a rural field setting. The first half of the poem describes "the sound of steel on stones" as the reapers "start their silent swinging, one by one." The second half contrasts this human activity with the sharp efficiency of a mechanical mower, which kills a field rat with machinelike precision and continues on its way. The contrast between the human and the mechanical emphasizes not only the displacement of black workers by machines, but also the passing of an era. The poem ends with a lament for the destruction of nature by the machine, "I see the blade,/Blood-stained, continue cutting weeds and shade."

Also written in iambic pentameter couplets, "November Cotton Flower" is a variation of the Italian sonnet. The octave depicts a late autumn setting, the end of the cotton season. Drought ravages the land as birds seek water in wells a hundred feet below the ground. The sestet describes the blooming of a November cotton flower amid this arid and barren scene, an event perceived to be supernatural by the local inhabitants, "Superstition saw/Something it had never seen before." The concluding couplet reveals the poem to be an extended metaphor, completing the analogy of the flower's mystery and sudden beauty in terms of a beautiful and spontaneous brown-eyed woman: "Brown eyes that loved without a trace of fear,/Beauty so sudden for that time of year." Like the November cotton flower, she is an anomaly within her depressed and rustic environment.

"Cotton Song" belongs to a subgenre of Afro-American folk songs that captures the agony and essence of slavery. The poet uses music—the work song itself—to symbolize the medium by which slaves transcended the vicissitudes of slavery. Moreover, it is precisely spiritual freedom that engenders thoughts of political freedom:

> Cotton bales are the fleecy way
> Weary sinner's bare feet trod,
> Softly, softly to the throne of God,
> "We ain't agwine t wait until th Judgement Day!"

"Song of the Son" and "Georgia Dusk" are swan songs for the passing Afro-American folk spirit. "Song of the Sun" develops in two movements, with images of sight, sound, and smell. The first movement evokes images of smoke and music. Once stately Georgia pines have been reduced to smouldering sawdust piles; smoke spiraling toward heaven is the by-product of their former grandeur. Similarly, the "parting soul" of the Black American folk experience has been reduced to an evening song which, like the smoke, carries throughout the valley of cane. The poet is imaged as the prodigal son, returning "just before an epoch's sun declines" to capture in art the fleeting legacy of a "song-lit race of slaves." The second movement develops as an extended metaphor of slaves as "dark purple ripened plums,/Squeezed, and bursting in the pine-wood air." The imagery recalls the cloying state of fruit as it passes into the oblivion of the postharvest. Yet the spectatorial poet is able to preserve "one plum" and "one seed" to immortalize both the past and the passing order in art.

In "Georgia Dusk" the sky relents to the setting sun and night in a "lengthened tournament for flashing gold." In this nocturnal setting, "moon and men and barking hounds" are engaged in "making folk-songs from soul sounds." As in "Song of the Son," wraiths of smoke from a "pyramidal sawdust pile" symbolize the passing of an era, supplanted by industry, "only chips and stumps are left to show/The solid proof of former domicile." With the advent of dusk, however, comes a heightened sense of the black man's union with the spiritual world, "with vestiges of pomp,/Race memories of king and caravan,/High-priests, ostrich, and a juju-man." These mystical moments inspire the people to sing; their voices resonate and travel throughout the piney woods and the valley of cane. The poem concludes with an invocation to the singers, "Give virgin lips to cornfield concubines,/Bring dreams of Christ to dusky cane-lipped throngs." The juxtaposition of secular and religious imagery symbolizes the mystical power of Afro-American folk music to harmonize the earthly (the "cornfield concubines" and "dusky cane-lipped throngs") and the heavenly ("sacred whisper," "virgin lips," and "dreams of Christ").

"Nullo," "Conversion," and "Portrait in Georgia" are Imagist in form and design. "Nullo" captures the fiery, iridescent beauty of golden, sun-drenched pine needles falling upon a cowpath in a forest at sunset. The poem effectively arrests the stillness and solitude of the moment: "Rabbits knew not of their falling,/Nor did the forest catch aflame." "Conversion" images the spirit of Afro-American culture—the "African Guardian of Souls"—as compromised and debased by western influences, "Drunk with rum,/Feasting on a strange cassava,/Yielding to new words and a weak palabra/Of a white-faced sardonic god." "Portrait in Georgia" is reminiscent of "Face," in which Toomer attempts to render a vision of the poem's title. This Georgian portrait, however, is one of a lynched and burned black woman:

> Breath—the last sweet scent of cane,
> And her slim body, white as the ash
> of black flesh after flame.

The sonnet "Beehive" discloses a shift in the poet's consciousness from spiritual identification to spiritual alienation. This lyric develops in two movements as an extended metaphor of the poet as exile in Eden. The first movement symbolizes the world as a black beehive, buzzing with activity on a moonlit, silvery night. The second movement, however, describes the spectatorial poet's estrangement, when he characterizes himself as an unproductive and exploiting drone, "Lipping honey,/Getting drunk with silver honey." Although he has tasted the "silver honey" of Afro-American culture, he is nevertheless unable to bridge the gap between himself and his fellow workers, unable to "fly out past the moon/And curl forever in some far-off farmyard flower."

"Prayer" describes a waning of the spirit and the creative powers, resulting from a dissociation of inner and outer, soul and body: "My body is opaque to the soul./Driven of the spirit, long have I sought to temper it unto the spirit's/longing,/But my mind, too, is opaque to the soul." This failure of the spirit, and of its creative powers, is reflected metapoetically in the lines "I am weak with much giving./I am weak with the desire to give more."[8]

Completing the mandalic or spiritual design, "Harvest Song" dramatizes the poet's loss of empathetic union with the essence of Afro-American culture and consciousness. Ironically titled, "Harvest Song" describes an artist's inability to become one with the subjects of his art, as well as an inability to transform the raw materials of his labor into art. Reminiscent of Robert Frost's "After Apple-Picking," "Harvest Song" develops as an extended portrait of the poet as reaper. Although the poet-reaper has successfully cradled the fruits of his labor, when he cracks a grain from the store of his cradled oats, he cannot taste its inner essence. In vain, he attempts to stare through time and space to understand the sources of his inspiration; he tries to make up the physical distance by straining to hear the calls of other reapers and their songs. But his dust-caked senses preclude any meaningful or helpful intervention. The "knowledge of hunger" he fears is the failure of consciousness and of the creative impulse. Thus he is reluctant to call other reapers for fear they will share their truly inspiring grains, grains he is unable to assimilate. "It would be good to hear their songs . . reapers of the sweet-stalk'd/cane, cutters of the corn . . even though their throats/cracked and the strangeness of their voices deafened me." Still, he beats his soft, sensitive palms against the stubble of the fields of labor, and his pain is sweeter and more rewarding than the harvest itself. He is then comforted by the pains of his struggles, although they will not bring him knowledge of his hunger.

A newly discovered poem of this period is the mystical and compelling "Tell Me," which contains imagery of nature evocative of the local color poems in *Cane*, although it was inspired by the majestic mountains and the scenic Shenandoah River near Harpers Ferry. Written in three four-line stanzas of rhymed iambic tetrameter, this poem unfolds with a series of apostrophes to the "dear beauty of the dusk," as the poet implores the spirit of nature to share with him its dark and mysterious essence.

III

Shortly after the publication of *Cane* in October 1923, Toomer began studying the austere idealism of the Greek-Armenian mystic, Georges Gurdjieff, and in 1924 he attended the Gurdjieff Institute for the Harmonious Development of Man at the Château de Prieuré in Fontainebleau, France. Toomer sailed back to America after two months, but returned to the Gurdjieff Institute in 1926, 1927, and 1929. Yet even with the rigorous demands engendered by his devotion to Gurdjieff, Toomer continued writing and assembling his poetry.[9] Indeed, as we shall see, poetry provided an artful medium for imaging his ideas on the phenomenology of "Objective Consciousness." While Gurdjieffian philosophy is arcane and obscure, we need not concern ourselves with its esoterica in order to formulate the major tenets as they relate to Toomer.[10] For purposes of examining the poetry written during this period, three questions must be addressed: the concept of the Absolute, the nature of consciousness, and the function of art.

Gurdjieff's concept of the Absolute is set forth in his Ray of Creation theory of the universe, which he uses to illustrate what he terms the Two Great Cosmic Laws of the universe, the Law of Three and the Law of Seven. According to Gurdjieff, the individual is a small model of the universe, made of the same materials and governed by the same rules. His Law of Three states that all phenomena, from the subatomic to the cosmic, result from the interaction of three principles or forces: two opposing forces, and a third which functions as a synthesis. Within the Absolute, however, these forces are supremely regulated and harmonized by "Will," "Full Consciousness," and "Understanding." It is this supreme force which is responsible for the creation of the universe. The Law of Seven describes the universe in terms of an immense network of energy radiations or vibrations. In accordance with this Law, the Ray of Creation was a "descending octave," much like the Great Chain of Being, with "intervals" that must be bridged if the continuous flow of energy radiations is to be maintained.

In terms of the nature of consciousness, the "ordinary man," Gurdjieff tells us, "is a three-brained being," his ontological status shared among three autonomous centers: physical, emotional, and intellectual. In some people the center of gravity is located in the moving center; in others in the intellectual or emotional center. Beyond these centers, however, there exist higher levels of objective consciousness, which Gurdjieff calls the "higher emotional center" and the "higher thinking center." On these levels of mystical awareness, the self is the recipient of a miraculous "energy" from a nonmaterial source in direct communion with the supernatural. In religious philosophy, this state of consciousness is called "illumination," "enlightenment," or "epiphany." In the words of Richard Gregg, "there is a blending of subject and object, a mutual absorption, a forgetting of everything else; there is often delight, and exaltation, an enthusiasm, a rapture, a deep and abiding joy. . . . It is not knowing from without; it is knowing from within. It is not knowing about; it is unitive knowledge. Unitive knowledge is much more complete and deeper than knowing about."[11] Within this realm of unitive knowledge, one is impressed not by the diversity of experience, but by its unity. Thus, the closer one gets to pure, objective consciousness, the more one finds one-self absorbed into a nameless entity immeasureably greater than the self. In this way, Gurdjieffian idealism posits the self as undifferentiated consciousness, energized by the Ray of Creation.

Finally, it is important to understand Gurdjieff's conception of art, particularly in light of an affective aesthetic that generally characterizes the poetry Toomer wrote during this period. Gurdjieff's art aesthetic is perhaps most clearly revealed in his theory of "Objective Art." "I measure the merit of art by its consciousness, you by its unconsciousness. A work of objective art is a book which transmits the artist's ideas not directly through words or signs or hieroglyphics but through feelings which he evokes in the beholder consciously and with full knowledge of what he is doing and why he is doing it."[12] In view of this aesthetic and its influence on Toomer, one would be correct in surmising that the poetry of this period was written to inspire higher consciousness. Yet we must also keep in mind that Toomer had already clearly declared his preference for affective over emotive art as early as 1921, in his review of "The Art of Poetry."

Toomer's Objective Consciousness poetry may be grouped into several categories: poems on being consciousness and self-integration, such as "The Lost Dancer," "Unsuspecting," and "White Arrow"; poems revealing mysticism and "New American" consciousness, such as "At Sea" and "The Gods Are Here," and "The Blue Meridian," respectively; poems of consciousness of the self that is the cosmos, as represented by "Peers" and "Living Earth," and poems on consciousness of the self that is humanity, as represented by "Men" and "People."

"The Lost Dancer" expresses the poet's quest for unity of being and self-integration in terms of the failure of idealism. The dancer-artist figure is "lost" because he is unable to discover a "source of magic" whereby he can transcend the rigorous imperatives of subject-object dualism—inner and outer, essence and personality, self and world, art and life—here symbolized by the metaphysical "vibrations of the dance" and the physical "feet dancing on earth of sand":

> Spatial depths of being survive
> The birth to death recurrences

Of feet dancing on earth of sand;
Vibrations of the dance survive
The sand; the sand, elect, survives
The dancer. He can find no source
Of magic adequate to bind
The sand upon his feet, his feet
Upon his dance, his dance upon
The diamond body of his being.

Unity of being then follows when the dancer is able to synthesize "the birth to death recurrences/Of feet dancing on earth of sand" (object), with "the diamond body of his being," the prismatic brilliance of inner essence (subject), to form a unified complex, the transcendental self.

"Unsuspecting" utilizes imagery borrowed from horticulture ("culls," "trims," and "prunes"), as well as reflexive rhyme ("mind" and "rind") to suggest that refined, cultivated intellect without corresponding inner development is naive and superficial.[13]

There is a natty kind of mind
That slicks its thoughts,
Culls its oughts,
Trims its views,
Prunes its trues,
And never suspects it is a rind.

Composed in iambic pentameter, "White Arrow" sketches the poet's Lawrentian notion of female self-actualization in contrasting images of sleeping or existing and waking or being, images drawn from the language of Gurdjieff's system. The poem unfolds as an affectionate admonition to an unnamed individual to liberate herself from the "sleep and fear" induced by the authority of gender socialization: "In faith and reason you were swift and free,/White arrow, as you were, awake and be!"

Both "At Sea" and "The Gods Are Here" are expressions of mystical experiences. "At Sea" dramatizes an ephemeral and fleeting moment during which the poet is transfixed by the awesome power and beauty of the sea. While in this mystical state of consciousness, he experiences a "pang of transience," when the spirit of the universe briefly reveals itself in the life and order of the cosmos:

> Once I saw large waves
> Crested with white-caps;
> A driving wind
> Transformed the caps
> Into scudding spray—
> "Swift souls," I addressed them—
> They turned towards me
> Startled
> Sea-descending faces;
> But I, not they,
> Felt the pang of transience.

"The Gods Are Here" develops as an extended contrast between two forms of asceticism, both of which release the soul from bondage and permit its union with the divine—that of the hermit on a mountain among the wilds of nature, and that of the poet within the domestic environment of society:

> This is no mountain
> But a house,
> No rock of solitude
> But a family chair,
> No wilds
> But life appearing
> As life anywhere domesticated,
> Yet I know the gods are here,
> And that if I touch them
> I will arise
> And take majesty into the kitchen.

A minor classic of American literature, "The Blue Meridian" is a Whitmanian affirmation of democratic idealism, a poetics of democracy.[14] In describing the original text of this poem, Toomer reveals his

"New American" or millennial consciousness. "I wrote a poem called 'The First American,' the idea of which was that here in America we are in the process of forming a new race, that I was one of the first conscious members of this race."[15] Toomer believed that his own blend of ethnic strains, like America's melting pot itself, conferred upon him a mystical selfhood and a transcendental vision of America. Like Walt Whitman, he believed that there is a central identity of self which is the foundation of freedom, that each individual is unique and yet identical with the all, and that democracy is the surest guarantee of individual values. And like Whitman he attempted to resolve the conflict between individual and society at the transpersonal level by positing his own self, "the first American," as the self of all beings. Toomer's Adamic conception of himself as one of the first conscious members of a united human race is the very cornerstone of his "First American" or "New American" consciousness. Such an exalted mind, carrying with it the conviction of absolute novelty, recalls the "Cosmic Consciousness" of Canadian psychologist R. M. Bucke. "Along with the consciousness of the cosmos," writes Bucke, "there occurs an intellectual enlightenment which alone would place the individual on a new plane of existence—would make him almost a member of a new species."[16] Having formulated an identity, Toomer as the new American Adam proceeds to become the maker of his own conditions by projecting a model society. According to R. W. B. Lewis, the American Adam *projects* a world of order and meaning and identity into either a chaos or a vacuum; he does not *discover* it."[17] This is precisely what Toomer does in "The Blue Meridian":

> When the spirit of mankind conceived
> A New World in America, and dreamed
> The human structure rising from this base,
> The land was as a vacant house to new inhabitants,
> A vacuum compelled by Nature to be filled.
> Spirit could not wait to time-select,
> Weighing in wisdom each piece,
> Fitting each right thing into each right place,
> But had to act, trusting the vision of the possible.

Of the poems Toomer wrote on consciousness of the self that is the cosmos, the most representative are "Peers" and "Living Earth." "Peers" opens with an apostrophe to nature, here symbolized by a rock. For the poet, however, the mutual existence of man and nature confirms their ontological status as peers:

> Some day I will see again
> Your substance in the sacred flame
> And meet you undisguised
> In the root of all that lives.

Similarly, Toomer compares the life and order of the universe with the life and order of man in "Living Earth":

> Is not Earth, Being,
> Is it not a core of Life,
> Has it not organisms with spine,
> Glands, entrails, and a sage navel?
> Is it not a field of Force,
> Force and field living?

Rejecting the idea that the earth is ruled by fate, blind force, and accident, the poet avers that the only conceivable accident is for mankind to attribute to the universe the blindness that is fixed within himself. The poem ends on a note of questioning consciousness in nature, as a first step in understanding consciousness in man.

A vision of universal brotherhood, "Men" affirms unity through diversity:

> Separate in bodies
> Many in desires
> One in ultimate reality
>
> Strangers on the earth
> Prisoners in this world
> Natives of deity

In like manner, "People" asserts the unity of humanity and the belief that individuals must use their inner eyes if they are to see beings instead of races:

> What odd passions,
> What queer beliefs
> That men who believe in sights
> Disbelieve in seers.

In addition to the Objective Consciousness poetry composed during this period, Toomer also wrote poems inspired by the landscape and culture of the American Southwest, particularly New Mexico. "Imprint for Rio Grande," "I Sit in My Room," "Rolling, Rolling," and "It Is Everywhere" represent a previously unrevealed dimension of Toomer as local colorist, depicting the natural beauty of the American Southwest and, as in "It Is Everywhere," a kaleidoscopic panorama of the American landscape.[18]

IV

In the summer of 1938 Toomer moved to Bucks County, Pennsylvania, where he was almost immediately attracted to Quakerism. During his apprenticeship with the Society of Friends, he immersed himself in Quaker religious philosophy, wrote numerous essays on George Fox and Quakerism, and, in 1940, joined the Society of Friends.[19] His interest in Quaker religious philosophy sprang from his own idea that the Society of Friends provided a radical venture beyond Objective Consciousness to a vital and transforming religious faith.

> Quakers assembled, I had been told, for silent worship and waited for the spirit to move them. This appealed to me because I had practiced meditation. Years before I had read a brief account of George Fox that impressed me. I had heard of the Quaker reputation for practicing what they preached ... Prior to coming into contact with Friends I had been convinced that God is both immanent and transcendent, and that the purpose of life is to grow up to

God; that within man there is a wonderful power that can transform him, lift him into new birth; that we have it in us to rise to a life wherein brotherhood is manifest and war impossible.[20]

To define the poetry of this period as Christian Existential, two factors must be considered. In the first place, Toomer envisioned Quaker religious philosophy as a bridge between two (Kierkegaardian) levels of consciousness, the ethical or social concerns of Objective Consciousness, and the religious or theistic concerns of Christianity. Indeed, in 1938 he sought to reconcile Gurdjieffian idealism with Quakerism by organizing a cooperative of both Quakers and lay individuals called Friends of Being. As we shall see, the ostensible conflict remains as the basis for a pervasive Christian Existentialism. In the second place, Quakerism and Christian Existentialism comprise fundamentally the same religious philosophy, both in contrast with Gurdjieffian idealism.[21] Thus in temperament and philosophy, Toomer's consciousness is best described as Christian Existential. And it is precisely this consciousness which is the genesis of his spiritual odyssey as a Quaker poet.

The meditative verses and confessional lyrics that comprise this period render a vision of man as alone, estranged from society, the universe, and God. Reflecting an evolution in the poet's spiritual consciousness, these poems fall into several categories: confessional lyrics manifesting subtle tensions between Objective Consciousness and Quaker Consciousness, as "Desire"; meditations for mediation between the self and God, such as "The Chase" and "Cloud"; confessional lyrics on asceticism, such as "Motion and Rest"; and lyrical verses of orthodox Quakerism, such as "To Gurdjieff Dying," "The Promise," and "They Are Not Missed."

In "Desire," conflicting claims of consciousness are imaged as two types and levels of love. The poem opens with religious allusions to "suffering" and "the opened heart," symbolic of the Sacred Heart. The imagery then shifts to reflect the poet's objective consciousness, "I seek the universal love of beings;/May I be made one with that love/And extend to everything;/I turn towards that love." This conflict between the ethical exigencies of agape and the moral concerns of Logos is conditionally reconciled in favor of the latter in the closing lines of this poem:

> In this new season of a forgotten life
> I move towards the heart of love
>   Of all that breathes;
> I would enter that radiant center
>   and from that center live.

The image of white birds in flight dramatizes the poet's quest for spiritual mediation in "The Chase":

> As the white bird leaves the dirty nest,
> Flashes in the dazzling sky,
> And merges in the blue,
> May my spirit quit me,
> And fly the beam straight
> Into thy power and thy glory.

"Cloud" employs a variation of the five line tanka to speculate on the "livid cloud" that separates man from the "salient light" of Quaker religious faith.

"Motion and Rest" images white birds coming to rest in a tranquil portrait of asceticism:

> I have watched white birds alight on
>   a barn roof
> And come to rest, instantly still,
>   effortlessly relaxed and poised,
> In them no trace of former motion.
>
> So would I come to rest, so should we
> Come to rest at quiet time.

Within the society of Friends, "Quietism" refers to a mystical state of consciousness wherein one experiences annihilation of the will and passive absorption into the Inner Light. The metaphor of motion and rest thus effectively dramatizes two contrasting states of consciousness: the realm of the world, with its social engagement, and the realm of the spirit, with its quietistic contemplation.

"To Gurdjieff Dying" is a carefully crafted Italian sonnet with varia-
tions in rhyme scheme. The poem employs end rhymes in the opening
and closing lines of both the octave and the sestet, with intermediate
iterating end rhymes, while retaining the conventions of iambic pentam-
eter. A profound repudiation of Gurdjieff, this sonnet demonstrates the
poet's devout acceptance of Quaker religious faith. The octave dispar-
ages Gurdjieff for "Knowing the Buddhic law but to pervert/Its power of
peace into dissevering fire." He is also described as a seducer "coiled as
a serpent round the phallic Tau/And sacramental loaf," and as a false
prophet, "Son of the Elder Liar." The sestet further reproves Gurdjieff
for having "deformed the birth-bringings of light/Into lust-brats of
black imaginings,/Spilling Pan-passions in the incarnate round/Of hell
and earth." The concluding lines invoke the "Lords of the Shining Rings/
Skilled in white magic," the authority of religion itself, to "save even
Gurdjieff from his hell forthright." Light and dark imagery here effec-
tively contrasts the "black imaginings" of Gurdjieffian idealism and the
"white magic" of religious faith.

"The Promise" reveals an acceptance of the paradox of religious faith
in contrasting images of spring in nature and "new birth" in man.
Whereas during the years of his earlier idealism Toomer had sought to
spread the gospel of pantheism and cosmic consciousness, here there is
manifested an essential disharmony between man and nature, and be-
tween man and God. That is, although "The cycles of the soul are sure as
those/Of sap," in nature seasonal cycles insure the eternal return of
spring, whereas in man there is no such guarantee, for he possesses the
will to seek union with God within. "It is not guaranteed that God,/
Coming from the south with light and love/Will touch the seed, melt
our crusts/And bestir Himself in us/When earth moves from cold to
warmth." Rather, in man the spirit must break free in a Kierkegaardian
leap of faith, before "Winter shall give way to spring within."

"They Are Not Missed" images God, time, and eternity in the context
of Old Testament religious faith. It opens with a series of metaphors,
suggesting that as old paths "forget the bruised feet," ancestral trees
"their fallen leaves," and old houses "The births and deaths that echo in/
Their rooms," God is similarly indifferent to the "souls who shared/His
glory once, long ago." That is, God, here described as "the ancient one,"
teleologically suspends the temporal in favor of the eternal. Like Abra-

ham in Kierkegaard's famous parable of the conflict between the claims of man and the claims of God, man must acquiesce to God's prudent and omniscient management of the universe. Indeed, in this poem there exists no tension between the ethical and the religious; rather, there is complete acceptance of man's responsibilities to "seek/Or sink . . . Till past and present meet, and time ends."

V

Toomer's poetry canon constitutes a study in the phenomena of the spirit, not only in its revelations of spiritualist philosophies—Orientalism, Afro-American mysticism, Gurdjieffian Idealism, and Quakerism—but in its formal expression of the poet's highest goals, to essentialize and spiritualize experience. "I am not a romanticist," writes Toomer, "I am not a classicist nor a realist, in the usual sense of these terms. I am an essentialist. Or, to put it in other words, I am a spiritualizer, a poetic realist. This means two things. I try to lift facts, things, happenings to the planes of rhythm, feeling, and significance. I try to clothe and give body to potentialities."[22] He describes the mystical ecstasy of poetic creation as an epiphany: "a flash bridges the gap between inner and outer, causing a momentary fusion and wholeness. Thus poetry starts, at least to me."[23] Finally, Toomer viewed poetry not merely as sheer aesthetic pleasure, but as a means of enlarging one's heart and consciousness. In his own words, "Poems are Offerings. Gifts to me I give to you."[24]

Robert B. Jones
Houston, Texas

NOTES

1. The individually published poems are "Song of the Son," *Crisis* 23, no. 6 (1922): 261; "Banking Coal," *Crisis* 24, no. 2 (1922): 65; "Georgia Dusk," *Liberator* 5, no. 9 (1922): 25; "Harvest Song," *Double Dealer* 4, no. 24 (1922): 258; "Gum," *Chapbook* 36 (1923): 22; "White Arrow," *Dial* 86 (1929): 596;

"Brown River, Smile," *Pagany* 3 (1932): 29–33; "As the Eagle Soars," *Crisis* 41, no. 41 (1932): 116; "[The] Blue Meridian" in *The New Caravan*, ed. Alfred Kreymborg, Lewis Mumford, and Paul Rosenfeld (New York: W. W. Norton and Company, 1936); "Imprint for Rio Grande," *New Mexico Sentinel*, 12 January 1938, p. 6; and "See the Heart," *Friends Intelligencer* 104 (1947): 423. "Five Vignettes," "The Lost Dancer," and "At Sea" appear in *Black American Literature: Poetry*, ed. Darwin Turner (Columbus, Ohio: Charles E. Merrill, 1969), while "And Pass," "Angelic Eve," "Honey of Being," "Sing Yes," "Men," "Peers," "Mended," and "One Within" were first published in *The Wayward and the Seeking*, ed. Darwin Turner (Washington, D.C.: Howard University Press, 1980). "Reapers," "Cotton Song," "Nullo," "Conversion," "Portrait in Georgia," "Beehive," and "Prayer" were first published in Jean Toomer, *Cane* (New York: Boni and Liveright, 1923). The unpublished poems, including a 1931 untitled collection, a 1934 volume entitled "The Blue Meridian and Other Poems," and the most comprehensive of the projected volumes, "The Wayward and the Seeking" (ca. 1940) are located in the Jean Toomer Collection, Box 50, Beinecke Rare Book and Manuscript Library, Yale University, New Haven, Conn.

2. Bernard Bell explores thematic relationships in "A Key to the Poems in *Cane*," *CLA Journal* 14 (March 1971): 251–58. Also, Michael Krasny examines selected poems in "Jean Toomer and the Quest for Consciousness" (Ph.D. diss., University of Wisconsin, 1972). Carolyn Taylor discusses the Mill House poems in light of Gurdjieffian philosophy in " 'Blend Us with Thy Being': Jean Toomer's Mill House Poems" (Ph.D. Diss., Boston College, 1977). Nellie McKay provides cogent analyses of the poems in *Cane* in *Jean Toomer, Artist* (Chapel Hill: University of North Carolina Press, 1984).

3. Jean Toomer, "Outline of an Autobiography," in *The Wayward and the Seeking*, ed. Turner, p. 119.

4. Ibid., p. 120.

5. See Richard Aldington, "The Art of Poetry" *Dial* 69 (1920): 167–80. In his review, Toomer extols the formal and technical precision of Imagist poetry before arguing philosophically that poetry should be moral as well as imitative. He takes exception to Aldington's assertion that "the old cant of a poet's 'message' is completely discredited," arguing eloquently that poets and readers of the Western world are more inspired by what he terms "the mighty voices of the past" than mere pictorial beauty. Toomer then chides those poets "whose eyes are so charmed and fascinated by the gem, by its outward appearance, by its external form, that the spirit behind the gem is not perceived." Thus while he adopts the formalism inherent in Pound's Doctrine of the Image, he rejects the Imagist prohibition of "message" as an integral part of the poem. Toomer's review may be located in the Jean Toomer Collection, Box 55, Folder 6.

6. Gertrude Stein, *Tender Buttons*, in *Selected Writings of Gertrude Stein*, ed. Carl Van Vechten (New York: Vintage Books, 1962), p. 461.

7. Jean Toomer to Waldo Frank, 12 December 1922, Jean Toomer Collection, Box 3, Folder 6. Retrospectively, Toomer viewed *Cane* as a "spiritual fusion" of his inner and his outer selves. "While my native instinct to dreams and reading built up that inner life by means of which the outer is transformed into works of art, by means of which the outer gets its deeper meaning, it must not be thought, however, that these two loves existed, as it were, side by side in a mutual and sustaining contract. For a long while just the opposite was true. Whichever was for the time being dominant would try to deny and cut off the other. And from this conflict a most distressing friction arose. In fact, only a year or so ago did they creatively come together. *Cane* is the first evidence of this fusion." Jean Toomer Collection, Box 64, Folder 15.

8. In a letter to Waldo Frank, dated 25 July 1922, Toomer confesses that "your letters, together with a bit of analysis on my part, have convinced me that the impulse which sprang from Sparta, Georgia, last fall has just about fulfilled and spent itself." Jean Toomer Collection, Box 3, Folder 6.

9. In 1931, Toomer assembled his poems in a loosely bound, untitled collection divided into three parts, the extended prose poem "Sing Yes," twenty-eight lyric poems, and "The Blue Meridian." During the next three years, he added eleven poems to his collection, deleted others, and rearranged the titles, retaining the overall tripartite structure. In 1934, he personally copyrighted the volume and entitled it "The Blue Meridian and Other Poems." Toomer projected two other volumes, both undated, "Day Will Come" (also entitled "Rise") and "As Hands Unturned." But by far the most complete and comprehensive of his projected volumes is "The Wayward and the Seeking," which contains seventy poems, including fifty new poems that do not appear in either of the earlier collections. Toomer divided this volume into seven parts:

I

"I See her Lovely There"   "The Lost Dancer"
"White Arrow"*   "This He Taught Me"
"Grace"*   "People"*
"It Used to Be"   "Men"*
"Wedger"*
"Wolf from Lamb"   II
"Mended"*   "Living Earth"*
"Peers"*   "Rhymes for Children"*
"One Within"*   "At Sea"
"Frozen Assets"*   "T.F.E."

*These poems appear in neither the 1931 nor the 1934 projected volumes.

10. The most comprehensive studies of Gurdjieff's philosophy are Kenneth Walker, *A Study of Gurdjieff's Teachings* (London: Jonathan Cape, 1957); Michel Waldberg, *Gurdjieff: An Approach to His Ideas*, trans. Steve Cox (London: Routledge and Kegan Paul, 1981); Daly King, *The Oragean Version* (New York: Privately printed, 1951); and P. D. Ouspensky, *In Search of the Miraculous* (New York: Harcourt Brace, 1949). In this context, see also Jean Toomer, "Why I Entered the Gurdjieff Work," Jean Toomer Collection, Box 66, Folder 8.

11. Kenneth Walker, *A Study of Gurdjieff's Teachings* (London: Jonathan Cape, 1957), pp. 49–50.

12. Ibid., p. 116.

13. Toomer studied agricultural science at the University of Wisconsin (1914), and at the Massachusetts College of Agriculture (1916). His own belief in the unity of man and nature is the basis for much of the mysticism in *Cane*, as well as for the Wordsworthian pantheism that characterizes the Objective Consciousness period.

14. Between the summer of 1920 and the fall of 1921, Toomer read Whitman's *The Complete Writings* as well as the available secondary criticism, chiefly on *Leaves of Grass*. It was during this period that he wrote drafts for "The First American," later revised as "Brown River, Smile," (1931) and finally revised as "The Blue Meridian" (1936). For discussions of "The Blue Meridian," see Jean Wagner, *Black Poets of the United States*, trans. Kenneth Douglas (Urbana, Ill.: University of Illinois Press, 1973), pp. 272–81; and Bernard Bell, "Jean Toomer's 'Blue Meridian': The Poet as Prophet of a New Order of Man," *Black American Literature Forum* 14, no. 2 (Summer 1980): 77–80.

15. Jean Toomer, "Outline of an Autobiography," in *The Wayward and the Seeking*, ed. Turner, pp. 120–21.

16. Richard M. Bucke, *Cosmic Consciousness: A Study in the Evolution of the Human Mind* (New York: E. P. Dutton, 1923), p. 38.

17. R. W. B. Lewis, *The American Adam* (Chicago: University of Chicago Press, 1955), p. 51.

18. In 1925 Mabel Dodge Luhan invited Toomer to visit Taos, New Mexico, and lecture on Gurdjieff's philosophy of harmonious development. Several years later, in 1934, he and Marjorie Content lived in Taos for several weeks following their marriage. In 1939, the Toomers drove from San Francisco to Santa Fe after returning from India. In the context of Toomer's writings, see Tom Quirk and Robert Fleming, "Jean Toomer's Contributions to *The New Mexico Sentinel*," *CLA Journal* 19, no. 4 (June 1976): 524–32.

19. During his apprenticeship with the Society of Friends, Toomer read voraciously—George Fox's *Journal*, Fox's epistles entitled *A Day Book of Counsel and Comfort*, Robert Barclay's *An Apology for the True Christian Divinity*,

William Penn's *Rise and Progress of the People called Quakers* and *No Cross, No Crown*, Issac Pennington's *Letters*, John Woolman's *Journal*, and Rufus Jones's multivolumed edition of the Quaker History Series.

20. Jean Toomer, "Why I Joined the Society of Friends," Jean Toomer Collection, Box 28, Folder 19.

21. See Jessamyn West, *The Quaker Reader* (New York: Viking Press, 1962), p. 25. According to West, "No quotations are necessary to show that there are likenesses between Quaker and existential thought. Quakers are Existential Christians, and Fox, though he had not the philosophical equipment of Sören Kierkegaard, attacked in his life the illusion against which Kierkegaard preached: 'the illusion that there is such a "thing" as Christianity, or that any "thing," be it creed, history, code or organization, can be Christian. Only the subjective individual can be a Christian.' Thus Richard Niebuhr describes Kierkegaard, and with the same words he might as truly have spoken of Fox. . . . Kierkegaard was in many respects waging Fox's battle two hundred years after Fox." Also see Howard Brinton, *The Religious Philosophy of Quakerism* (Wallingford, Pa.: Pendle Hill Publications, 1973), p. 29.

22. Jean Toomer, "Reflections of an Earth-Being," in *The Wayward and the Seeking*, ed. Turner, p. 20.

23. Jean Toomer, "Poetry and Spiritual Rebirth," Jean Toomer Collection, Box 25, Folder 20.

24. Ibid. In an oral history interview with Ann Shockley (24 October 1970), Marjorie Content Toomer notes that Toomer abandoned his career as a writer in 1955. My own research corroborates Mrs. Toomer's assertion. Jean Toomer died on 30 March 1967.

EDITORS' NOTE

This volume includes not only those works that demonstrate Toomer's formal mastery of the art of poetry, but also those poems which, while perhaps less artful, nevertheless illuminate Toomer's intellectual and philosophical development. In all cases, we have attempted to preserve the original orthography, punctuation, and formal arrangement of the individual poems.

THE AESTHETIC PERIOD

(1919–1921)

FIVE VIGNETTES

1

The red-tiled ships you see reflected,
Are nervous,
And afraid of clouds.

2

There, on the clothes-line
Still as she pinned them,
Pieces now the wind may wear.

3

The old man, at ninety,
Eating peaches,
Is he not afraid of worms?

4

Wear my thimble of agony
And when you sew,
No needle points will prick you.

5

In Y. Don's laundry
A Chinese baby fell
And cried as any other.

STORM ENDING

Thunder blossoms gorgeously above our heads,
Great, hollow, bell-like flowers,
Rumbling in the wind,
Stretching clappers to strike our ears . .
Full-lipped flowers
Bitten by the sun
Bleeding rain
Dripping rain like golden honey—
And the sweet earth flying from the thunder.

AND PASS

When the sun leaves dusk
On far horizons,
And night envelops
Empty seas
And fading dream-ships;
When the stars have eyes,
And their light blends
With darkness—
    I stand alone,
    Salute and pass
    Proud shadows.

HER LIPS ARE COPPER WIRE

whisper of yellow globes
gleaming on lamp-posts that sway
like bootleg licker drinkers in the fog

and let your breath be moist against me
like bright beads on yellow globes

telephone the power-house
that the main wires are insulate

(her words play softly up and down
dewy corridors of billboards)

then with your tongue remove the tape
and press your lips to mine
till they are incandescent

I SEE HER LOVELY THERE

Lord take her to a distant place,
Inaccessible to my fate,
That my pride may not break
Against her anviled loveliness.

That my face may not flake,
That my knees may not bend
That my feet may not slave,
That my brain may not flame—

Stop! Lord I see her lovely there,
Within me though in far-off space,
Lovelier than were she here,
And all I am is forced to yield.

Lord bring her from that distant place,
Inaccessible to my fate,
That my heart may break and break
Against her anviled loveliness.

EVENING SONG

Full moon rising on the waters of my heart,
Lakes and moon and fires,
Cloine tires,
Holding her lips apart.

Promises of slumber leaving shore to charm the moon,
Miracle made vesper-keeps,
Cloine sleeps,
And I'll be sleeping soon.

Cloine, curled like the sleepy waters where the moon-waves start,
Radiant, resplendently she gleams,
Cloine dreams,
Lips pressed against my heart.

FACE

Hair—
silver-gray,
like streams of stars,
Brows—
recurved canoes
quivered by the ripples blown by pain,
Her eyes—
mist of tears
condensing on the flesh below
And her channeled muscles
are cluster grapes of sorrow
purple in the evening sun
nearly ripe for worms.

A I R

Darts, touches much—flies, soars, hovers, puffs, breezes, blasts,
At its best with a "light touch," humor
Inflaters
"I'll try anything once." In this sense, wide tasters or experimenters.
Plain or colorless (or natural).

EARTH

Solid—stolid
"There"
Stay put, and, at the same time, it can
Travel, that is,
Move about through the world of things.
Dependable, from a physical point of view.

FIRE

Flickers, flames, burns.
Burns into a thing—hence, depth, profundity.
"Hot after something,"
Sparking, flowing, "in a fever"
Always stewing smoking panting
Flashy.

WATER

Flows—on and on. Soaks, bathes, slops, gushes.
It needs a container.
Seems not to be affected by impressions and experiences.
Saved from monotony by the ripples and currents of its flow.
    Plain—sameness.

POEM IN C

Go and see Carlowitz the Carthusian,
Then pray bring the cartouche and place it
On this cashmere, while I tell a story.
The steaming casserole passed my way
While I reclined beneath Castalay,
Dreaming, ye Gods, of castor oil.
There behind us lay the sombre catacombs
Ready to catapult their dead
Among us living catilines and caterans;
"Needest thou catharsis?" I asked the first.
"Nay," said he, "my place of birth was
Ancient famed Cathay, whence go roads
To the flaming cauldron, which has
Long since cavorted me. Thank you for
Your offer of service, but I, once upon a time
The Golden Caymen, need none of it."
Whereon, I caveated and took me home,
There to smell the sweet celandine.

SOUND POEM (1)

Mon sa me el kirimoor,
Ve dice kor, korrand ve deer,
Leet vire or sand vite,
Re sive tas tor;
Tu tas tire or re sim bire,
Rozan dire ras to por tantor,
Dorozire, soron,
Bas ber vind can sor, gosham,
Mon sa me el, a som on oor.

SOUND POEM (II)

Vor cosma saga
Vor reeshen flaga
Vor gorden maga
Vor shalmer raga

SKYLINE

A cow-hoof imprint
pressed against the under-asphalt of
Fifth Avenue, sustains it

the osseous teat of an inverted cow
spurts *s k y s c r a p e r s*
against a cloud
racing to
dusk,
and
it
sprays
　　　in
　　　　num
　　　　　　er
　　　　　　ab
　　　　　　le
blunt peaks against
the milky-way.

GUM

On top of two tall buildings,
   Where Seventh Street joints
The Avenue,
The city's signs:

                STAR
              J E S U S
         The Light of the World

                  .   .   .

              WRIGLEYS
                eat it
                  after
                    every meal
             It Does You Good

Intermittently, their lights flash
Down upon the streets of Washington,
The sleek pat streets some asphalt spider
Spun and tired of.
Upon a fountain in the square
Where sparrows get their water,
Upon the tambourines and drum
Of the Salvation Army jawing,
Hallelujah!
The crowd
         jaws Jesus
            jawing gum.

DELIVERED AT THE KNIGHTING
OF LORD DURGLING
BY
GREAT BRUCE-JEAN

This Durgling was a dual personage,
Old man Durgling, and young Davey Durgling.
Old man Durgling sat with a piqued bored face
And gazed at the show with eyes withering;
Then, with injured petulance he deigned to speak,
Whereon young Davy Durgling spoke up and said,
"Shut up, go to hell, shut up, shut up
You old slant whiskers, you old bored grouch,
Go kick yourself and be chased by cats,
The world is full of sweet-lipped interests,
Not to mention hot-lipped interests, and
Transcendental polygons are the forms of breasts."

BANKING COAL

Whoever it was who brought the first wood and coal
To start the Fire, did his part well;
Not all wood takes to fire from a match,
Nor coal from wood before it's burned to charcoal.
The wood and coal in question caught a flame
And flared up beautifully, touching the air
That takes a flame from anything.

Somehow the fire was furnaced,
And then the time was ripe for some to say,
"Right banking of the furnace saves the coal."
I've seen them set to work, each in his way,
Though all with shovels and with ashes,
Never resting till the fire seemed most dead;
Whereupon they'd crawl in hooded night-caps
Contentedly to bed. Sometimes the fire left alone
Would die, but like as not spiced tongues
Remaining by the hardest on till day would flicker up,
Never strong, to anyone who cared to rake for them.
But roaring fires never have been made that way.
I'd like to tell those folks that one grand flare
Transferred to memory tissues of the air
Is worth a life, or, for dull minds that turn in gold,
All money ever saved by banking coal.

THE ANCESTRAL

CONSCIOUSNESS PERIOD

(1921–1923)

REAPERS

Black reapers with the sound of steel on stones
Are sharpening scythes. I see them place the hones
In their hip-pockets as a thing that's done.
And start their silent swinging, one by one.
Black horses drive a mower through the weeds.
And there, a field rat, startled, squealing bleeds.
His belly close to ground. I see the blade,
Blood-stained, continue cutting weeds and shade.

NOVEMBER COTTON FLOWER

Boll-weevil's coming, and the winter's cold,
Made cotton-stalks look rusty, season's old,
And cotton, scarce as any southern snow,
Was vanishing; the branch, so pinched and slow,
Failed in its function as the autumn rake;
Drouth fighting soil had caused the soil to take
All water from the streams; dead birds were found
In wells a hundred feet below the ground—
Such was the season when the flower bloomed.
Old folks were startled, and it soon assumed
Significance. Superstition saw
Something it had never seen before:
Brown eyes that loved without a trace of fear,
Beauty so sudden for that time of year.

COTTON SONG

Come, brother, come. Lets lift it;
Come now, hewit! roll away!
Shackles fall upon the Judgment Day
But lets not wait for it.

God's body's got a soul,
Bodies like to roll the soul,
Cant blame God if we dont roll,
Come, brother, roll, roll!

Cotton bales are the fleecy way
Weary sinner's bare feet trod,
Softly, softly to the throne of God,
"We aint agwine t wait until th Judgment Day!

Nassur; nassur,
Hump.
Eoho, eoho, roll away!
We aint agwine t wait until th Judgment Day!"

God's body's got a soul,
Bodies like to roll the soul,
Cant blame God if we dont roll,
Come, brother, roll, roll!

SONG OF THE SON

Pour O pour that parting soul in song,
O pour it in the sawdust glow of night,
Into the velvet pine-smoke air tonight,
And let the valley carry it along.
And let the valley carry it along.

O land and soil, red soil and sweet-gum tree,
So scant of grass, so profligate of pines,
Now just before an epoch's sun declines
Thy son, in time, I have returned to thee.
Thy son, I have in time returned to thee.

In time, for though the sun is setting on
A song-lit race of slaves, it has not set;
Though late, O soil, it is not too late yet
To catch thy plaintive soul, leaving, soon gone,
Leaving, to catch thy plaintive soul soon gone.

O Negro slaves, dark purple ripened plums,
Squeezed, and bursting in the pine-wood air,
Passing, before they stripped the old tree bare
One plum was saved for me, one seed becomes

An everlasting song, a singing tree,
Caroling softly souls of slavery,
What they were, and what they are to me,
Caroling softly souls of slavery.

GEORGIA DUSK

The sky, lazily disdaining to pursue
  The setting sun, too indolent to hold
  A lengthened tournament for flashing gold,
Passively darkens for night's barbeque,

A feast of moon and men and barking hounds.
  An orgy for some genius of the South
  With blood-hot eyes and cane-lipped scented mouth,
Surprised in making folk-songs from soul sounds.

The sawmill blows its whistle, buzz-saws stop,
  And silence breaks the bud of knoll and hill,
  Soft settling pollen where plowed lands fulfill
Their early promise of a bumper crop.

Smoke from the pyramidal sawdust pile
  Curls up, blue ghosts of trees, tarrying low
  Where only chips and stumps are left to show
The solid proof of former domicile.

Meanwhile, the men, with vestiges of pomp,
  Race memories of king and caravan,
  High-priests, an ostrich, and a juju-man,
Go singing through the footpaths of the swamp.

Their voices rise . . the pine trees are guitars,
  Strumming, pine-needles fall like sheets of rain . .
  Their voices rise . . the chorus of the cane
Is caroling a vesper to the stars . .

O singers, resinous and soft your songs
  Above the sacred whisper of the pines,
  Give virgin lips to cornfield concubines,
Bring dreams of Christ to dusky cane-lipped throngs.

NULLO

A spray of pine-needles,
Dipped in western horizon gold,
Fell onto a path.
Dry moulds of cow-hoofs.
In the forest.
Rabbits knew not of their falling,
Nor did the forest catch aflame.

CONVERSION

African Guardian of Souls,
Drunk with rum,
Feasting on a strange cassava,
Yielding to new words and a weak palabra
Of a white-faced sardonic god—
Grins, cries
Amens,
Shouts hosanna.

PORTRAIT IN GEORGIA

Hair—braided chestnut,
coiled like a lyncher's rope,
Eyes—fagots,
Lips—old scars, or the first red blisters,
Breath—the last sweet scent of cane,
And her slim body, white as the ash
      of black flesh after flame.

BEEHIVE

Within this black hive to-night
There swarm a million bees;
Bees passing in and out the moon,
Bees escaping out the moon,
Bees returning through the moon,
Silver bees intently buzzing,
Silver honey dripping from the swarm of bees
Earth is a waxen cell of the world comb,
And I, a drone,
Lying on my back,
Lipping honey,
Getting drunk with silver honey,
Wish that I might fly out past the moon
And curl forever in some far-off farmyard flower.

PRAYER

My body is opaque to the soul.
Driven of the spirit, long have I sought to temper it unto the spirit's
  longing,
But my mind, too, is opaque to the soul.
A closed lid is my soul's flesh-eye.
O Spirits of whom my soul is but a little finger,
Direct it to the lid of its flesh-eye.
I am weak with much giving.
I am weak with the desire to give more.
(How strong a thing is the little finger!)
So weak that I have confused the body with the soul,
And the body with its little finger.
(How frail is the little finger.)
My voice could not carry to you did you dwell in stars,
O Spirits of whom my soul is but a little finger . .

HARVEST SONG

I am a reaper whose muscles set at sundown. All my oats are
   cradled.
But I am too chilled, and too fatigued to bind them. And I hunger.

I crack a grain between my teeth. I do not taste it.
I have been in the fields all day. My throat is dry. I hunger.

My eyes are caked with dust of oatfields at harvest-time.
I am a blind man who stares across the hills, seeking stack'd fields
   of other harvesters.

It would be good to see them . . crook'd, split, and iron-ring'd
   handles of the scythes. It would be good to see them,
   dust-caked and blind. I hunger.

(Dusk is a strange fear'd sheath their blades are dull'd in.)
My throat is dry. And should I call, a cracked grain like the
   oats . . . eoho—

I fear to call. What should they hear me, and offer me their
   grain, oats, or wheat, or corn? I have been in the fields all
   day. I fear I could not taste it. I fear knowledge of my hunger.

My ears are caked with dust of oatfields at harvest-time.
I am a deaf man who strains to hear the calls of other harvesters
   whose throats are also dry.

It would be good to hear their songs . . reapers of the sweet-stalk'd
   cane, cutters of the corn . . even though their throats
   cracked and the strangeness of their voices deafened me.

I hunger. My throat is dry. Now that the sun has set and I am
   chilled, I fear to call. (Eoho, my brothers!)

I am a reaper, (Eoho!) All my oats are cradled. But I am too
   fatigued to bind them. And I hunger. I crack a grain. It
   has no taste to it. My throat is dry . . .

O my brothers, I beat my palms, still soft, against the stubble of my
harvesting. (You beat your soft palms, too.) My pain is
sweet. Sweeter than the oats or wheat or corn. It will not
bring me knowledge of my hunger.

TELL ME

Tell me, dear beauty of the dusk,
  When purple ribbons bind the hill,
  Do dreams your secret wish fulfill,
Do prayers, like kernels from the husk

Come from your lips? Tell me if when
  The mountains loom at night, giant shades
  Of softer shadow, swift like blades
Of grass seeds come to flower. Then

Tell me if the night winds bend
  Them towards me, if the Shenandoah
  As it ripples past your shore,
Catches the soul of what you send.

THE OBJECTIVE

CONSCIOUSNESS PERIOD

(1924–1939)

THE LOST DANCER

Spatial depths of being survive
The birth to death recurrences
Of feet dancing on earth of sand;
Vibrations of the dance survive
The sand; the sand, elect, survives
The dancer. He can find no source
Of magic adequate to bind
The sand upon his feet, his feet
Upon his dance, his dance upon
The diamond body of his being.

HONEY OF BEING

Always your heart, atomic symbol,
Wherein experience returns
To essence and I know source
And end identical; your love,
Reason and creativeness,
Perfect, our aspirations seek,
And, having found, in ecstasy
Fold their wings upon fulfillment.

ANGELIC EVE

Strong threads have bound your starry life
Within a silver-silken chrysalis,
The world's prize,
   And its first object of envy.
Strong hands have shaded your clear sight
Within luxurious slumber,
Where, safe from the white solar
And the black sun of night,
   You have been kept virginal.
But now, though I am unskilled in magic,
Too blunt a key to unlock souls,
You stir, and your waking life
Makes my eyes luminous to see
   Angelic Eve,
The silk as wings upon her feet,
Emerging from undifferentiated air.

MERL

The waves know rocks by foam and recklessness,
An eager wish to make a long sand beach;
The gulls know waves by silver wriggling streaks,
The air is sensitive to gulls. As These,
I know Maine and her—trees evergreen,
Pine, spruce, and fir; a clear cool dawn,
A swelling sea, and rocks, great grey shoulders
Hunched, strong against the free wild waves;
I see Merl standing there, her hair
Rimmed by spray and rainbowed by sunshine.

WHITE ARROW

Your force is greater than your use of it.
Existing, yet you dream that breath depends
On bonds I once contracted for. It is
A false belief induced by sleep and fear.
In faith and reason you were swift and free,
White arrow, as you were, awake and be!

UNSUSPECTING

There is a natty kind of mind
That slicks its thoughts,
Culls its oughts,
Trims its views,
Prunes its trues,
And never suspects it is a rind.

THE GODS ARE HERE

This is no mountain
But a house,
No rock of solitude
But a family chair,
No wilds
But life appearing
As life anywhere domesticated,
Yet I know the gods are here,
And that if I touch them
I will arise
And take majesty into the kitchen.

AT SEA

Once I saw large waves
Crested with white-caps;
A driving wind
Transformed the caps
Into scudding spray—
"Swift souls," I addressed them—
They turned towards me
Startled
Sea-descending faces;
But I, not they,
Felt the pang of transience.

UPWARD IS THIS ACTUALITY

Upward is this Actuality,
Octaves beyond the idols
Aspired to in biped picturing.
Not Jacob pillowed on the rock
Could dream this prospect—
I walk through the Universe . . .
Beholding marble as emanation,
Love and ashes, the first pure dust,
And One, perfected striver,
The bridegroom of the cross,
Conveys the dart
To crack this gravestone.

It takes a well-spent lifetime, and perhaps more, to crystallize in us
    that for which we exist.
Let your doing be an exercise, not an exhibition.
Man is a nerve of the cosmos, dislocated, trying to quiver into place.
A true individual is not conformative but formative.
We move and hustle but lack rhythm.
We should have a living spirit and the ability to spiritualize experience.
We do not suffer: seldom does our essence suffer, but pride, vanity,
    egotism suffer in us.
My breathing is the Great Breath broken into nostrils.
Whatever is, is sacred.

BE WITH ME

I hoped that you
Would help me tap the second stream
And reverse my steps, the ages
I have walked away
Seeking I knew not what.

You did not fail me;
To the second station I did not arise,
Hearing the strange accents
Of our native language
    While those around me
    Call me dead.

Dead to the first
I live to the second;
And when I die where now I live,
And all these people call me dead,
    Do you, dark sister,
    Not forsake me.

THE BLUE MERIDIAN

It is a new America,
To be spiritualized by each new American.

Black Meridian, black light,
Dynamic atom-aggregate,
Lay sleeping on an inland lake.

Lift, lift, thou waking forces!
Let us feel the energy of animals,
The force of rumps and bull-bent heads
Crashing the barrier to man.
It must spiral on!
A million million men, or twelve men,
Must crash the barrier to the next higher form.

Beyond plants are animals,
Beyond animals is man,
Beyond man is the universe.

The Big Light,
Let the Big Light in!

O thou, Radiant Incorporeal,
The I of earth and of mankind, hurl
Down these seaboards, across this continent,
The thousand-rayed discus of thy mind,
And above our walking limbs unfurl
Spirit-torsos of exquisite strength!

The Mississippi, sister of the Ganges,
Main artery of earth in the western world,
Is waiting to become
In the spirit of America, a sacred river,
Whoever lifts the Mississippi
Lifts himself and all America;
Whoever lifts himself
Makes that great brown river smile.

The blood of earth and the blood of man
Course swifter and rejoice when we spiritualize.

We—priest, clown, scientist, technician,
Artist, rascal, worker, lazybones,
This is the whole—
Individuals and people,
This is the whole that stood with Adam
And has come down to us,
Never to be less,
Whatever side is up, however viewed,
Whatever the vicissitudes,
The needs of evolution that bring
Emphasis upon a part—
Man himself, his total body and soul,
This is the moving whole.

Men of the East, men of the West,
Men in life, men in death,
Americans and all countrymen—
Growth is by admixture from less to more,
Preserving the great granary intact,
Through cycles of death and life,
Each stage a pod,
Perpetuating and perfecting
An essence identical in all,
Obeying the same laws, unto the same goal,
That far-distant objective,
By ways both down and up,
Down years ago, now struggling up.

So lift, lift, thou waking forces!

The old gods, led by an inverted Christ,
A shaved Moses, a blanched Lemur,
And a moulting Thunderbird,
Withdrew into the distance and died,

Their dust and seed drifting down
To fertilize the seven regions of America.

We are waiting for a new God.
For revelation in our day,
For growth towards faceless Deity.

The old peoples—
The great European races sent wave after wave
That washed the forests, the earth's rich loam,
Grew towns with the seeds of giant cities,
Made roads, laid silver rails,
Sang of their swift achievement,
And perished, displaced by machines,
Smothered by a world too huge for little men,
Too empty for life to breathe in.
They say that near the end
It was a world of crying men and hard women,
A city of goddamn and Jehovah
Baptized in finance
Without benefit of saints,
Of dear defectives
Winnowing their likenesses from synthetic rock
Sold by national organizations of undertakers.

Someone said:
    Blood cannot mix with the stuff upon our boards
    As water with flour to make bread,
    Nor have we yeast, nor have we fire.
    Not iron, not chemicals or money
    Are animate to suffer and rejoice,
    Not what we have become, this angel-dough,
    But slowly die, never attaining birth
    Above the body, above its pain and hungers,
    To beat pavements, stand in lines,
    Fill space and drive motor-cars.

Another cried:
   It is because of thee, O Life,
   That the first prayer ends in the last curse.

Another sang:
   Late minstrels of the restless earth,
   No muteness can be granted thee,
   Lift thy laughing energies
   To that white point which is a star.

The great African races sent a single wave
And singing riplets to sorrow in red fields,
Sing a swan song, to break rocks
And immortalize a hiding water boy.

   I'm leaving the shining ground, brothers,
   I sing because I ache,
   I go because I must,
   I'm leaving the shining ground;
   Don't ask me where,
   I'll meet you there,
   Brothers, I am leaving the shining ground.

   But we must keep keep keep
      the watermelon.
   He moaned, O Lord, Lord,
   This bale will break me—
   But we must keep keep keep
      the watermelon—

The great red race was here.
In a land of flaming earth and torrent-rains,
Of red sea-plains and majestic mesas,
At sunset from a purple hill
The Gods came down;
They serpentined into pueblo,

And a white-robed priest
Danced with them five days and nights;
But pueblo, priest, and Shalakos
Sank into the sacred earth
To fertilize the seven regions of America.

Hé-ya, hé-yo, hé-yo,
Hé-ya, hé-yo, hé-yo,
The ghosts of buffaloes,
A lone eagle feather,
An untamed Navajo,
Hé-ya, hé-yo, hé-yo
Hé-ya, hé-yo, hé-yo.

We are waiting for a new people,
For the joining of men to men
And man to God.

When the spirit of mankind conceived
A New World in America, and dreamed
The human structure rising from this base,
The land was as a vacant house to new inhabitants,
A vacuum compelled by Nature to be filled.
Spirit could not wait to time-select,
Weighing in wisdom each piece,
Fitting each right thing into each right place,
But had to act, trusting the vision of the possible,
Had to bring vast life to this vast plot,
Drawing, in waves of inhabitation,
All the peoples of the earth,
Later to weed out, organize, assimilate.
And thus we are—
Gathered by the snatch of accident,
Selected with the speed of fate,
The alien and the belonging,
All belonging now,
Not yet made one and aged.

O thou, Radiant Incorporeal,
The I of earth and of mankind, hurl
Down these seaboards, across this continent,
The thousand-rayed discus of thy mind,
And blend our bodies to one flesh,
And blend this body to mankind.

The east coast is masculine,
The west coast is feminine,
The middle region is the child—
Reconciling force
And generator of symbols.

   Thou, great fields, waving thy growths
      across the world,
   Couldst thou find the seed which started thee?
   Can you remember the first great hand to sow?
   Have you memory of His intention?
   Great plains, and thou, mountains,
   And thou, stately trees, and thou,
   America, sleeping and producing with the
      seasons,
   No clever dealer can divide,
   No machine or scheme can undermine thee.

The prairie's sweep is flat infinity,
The city's rise is perpendicular to farthest star,
I stand where the two directions intersect,
At Michigan Avenue and Walton Place,
Level with my countrymen,
Right-angled to the universe.

It is a new America,
To be spiritualized by each new American.
To be taken as a golden grain
And lifted, as the wheat of our bodies,
To matter uniquely man.

I would give my life to see inscribed
Upon the arch of our consciousness
These aims: Growth, Transformation, Love,
That we might become heart-centered towards
　　　one another,
Love-centered towards God, dedicated to the creation
　　　of a higher type of man, growing up to Him.
Let new eyes see this statue in the bay,
Let this be quarantine to unbend dreams,
Let old eyes see it in Wall Street and the Loop,
And through this clearing house
Let all pass checks who may.

But out of our past comes hell,
Rushing us, sweeping us,
Winding us, blinding us,
Mistakes and hates,
Habits, blights, and greeds,
Out of our past they come
And they are hell.

The eagle, you should know, American,
Is a sublime and bloody bird,
A living dynamo
Capable of spiritualizing and sensualizing,
One or the other predominantly;
Its spread from tip to tip denotes extremes
Of affirming and denying,
Creating, destroying—
And the majestic flight may disappear;
Now we have become air-minded, it seems,
The eagle is a flying-machine,
One wing is broken,
The plunge to earth is panic before death.
There is force gone wrong.
Somewhere in our land, in cellars or banks,
In our souls there is a forgotten trust—

What is it we stamp upon our money?
May we stamp it upon ourselves
  In God We Trust.

  In one of the depression years,
  Or was it a prosperity year?
  I forget. I forget, too, whether the
  Republicans were in, the Democrats out,
  Or vice versa. At any rate, it was during
  The time of man, and some said everything was
  All right, and some said just the reverse,
  That I met a girl upon the streets—
  "So you are, eh, ready, ready for anything,
  A fly little bum? It's OK with me.
  Let's go to a night club
  Where we men who disembowel the day
  Drink and coax reluctant lust,
  Come jazz. Make the place as swank as you like,
  I've got millions, they all know me,
  And, kid, who knows, it may be
  Our luck to see the dancing Wow,
  The rage of this old town, the one
  The everybody's crazy about,
  I said the Wow,
  The Bold Bitch of Babylon."
  I got a surprise, believe me I did,
  She replied—
  "Yes, I too have let friends suffer for a day,
  But never always. I see yesterday and tomorrow,
  From me are drawn the powers that heal,
  Sweeten, give new faith and make us remember
  That to live is to grow, to grow is to love,
  And this is what we are here to do.
  You, then, must convince me that you know
  The undying seed and its destiny,
  The yesterday before birth, the after-death
    tomorrow,

The now of man and woman—
So will I believe you worthy to let me."

(The nature that man should have, and woman,
The trust and faith in one another,
The depth and beauty of relationship—
That after chaos they may manifest again
And build their worlds.)

An airplane, with broken wing,
In a tail-spin,
Descends with terrifying speed—
"Don't put me on the spot!"—
From beings to nothings,
From human beings to grotesques,
From men and women to manikins,
From forms to chaoses—

Crash!

Of what avail that with neon lights
We make gas-tanks look like Christmas trees?
Of what avail the battle
Of the school-books and the guns?
What use bombs and anti-bombs,
Sovereign powers, brutal lives, ugly deaths?
Are men born to go down like this?
Violence is violence.
Our holidays leave us as we were,
Our schools do not regenerate,
Precisely the educated are the brains of war,
Our churches do not transform—
So here we are. In war, in peace

Blood does not mix with the stuff upon our boards,
As water with flour to make bread,
Nor have we yeast, nor have we fire.

Not steel, not chemicals or money
Are spirited to suffer and rejoice,
Not what we have become, this angel-dough,
But slowly die, never having birth
Above the body, above its ego and hungers,
To sit at desks, stand in lines, ask for jobs,
Fill space and pass time
Within a prison system all of wardens.

Nor does it help to know that thus
The pioneers and puritans have legacied us,
They, indentured to all men before them.

Nor can we eat, though food is here,
Nor can we breathe, though the world is air,
Nor can we move, though the planet speeds,
Nor can we circulate, though Nature flows,
Nor can we love and bear love's fruit
Though we are living and life is everywhere.

It is because of thee, O Man,
That the first prayer ends in the last curse.

In truth, in no ordinary way
Can anyone quit any racket.

Men and women—
It begins with us,
So we must end it.

On what vermilion peak will squad-cars cluster
When the universe sounds judgment-day,
Vigilant for what gong-alarm
To get what anti-cosmic outlaws?
Down what rosy-golden streets will the black cars
    cruise,
Watchful for what syndicate

Of racketeers and hijackers,
And where the bull-pen, what the bars,
And who the men who will thus help God?

Men,
Men and women—
Liberate!

Yet, in this crashing world
Terrorized by bullet-athletes,
I unbolt windows and ten-cents greet
A happy simple thing—
An organ grinder with jaunty hat,
With wayward roaming feet,
And his monkey,
Sauntering along a spring street,
Diddle-lidle-le, diddle-lidle-le.

Late minstrels of the restless earth,
No muteness can be granted thee,
Lift thy laughing energies
To that white point which is a star.

There is land—I have worked it with my hands,
There are materials for every known and unknown need of man,
There are houses built and more to build,
Calling to the creator in each person,
There are men, there are women,
There are all the coming generations,
There is Life—but,
On land are shadows not of trees or clouds,
On materials marks not made by Nature,
On men and women ravages no animal could make,
On children brands,
On life a blight not put by God—
Gargoyle shadows,
Finger marks,

Ghosts like us,
A blight in an image recognized,
I having seen myself—
O Man, that thy mask
Streaks the space between the sun and earth,
Streaks the air between thyself and thyself.

Driven by what the cosmos has put in me
Let me then affirm to those, the mazed,
Who like myself have seen self-streaks,
Who too have felt the sear
And would rather suffer it than pass it on—
We are made to grow, and by growing attain,
Rising in new birth to live in love.
The brotherhood of man cannot be realized
By stunted men, nor by those dismembered,
Closed in themselves, cut off from the mainstream
And therefore frustrated and bent to live in hate;
Exiles can but gang against themselves and earth,
Suffering the wrong turn as it works out
With ever stronger compulsion towards catastrophe.
We who would transform ex-I to I
And move from outlaw to I AM,
May know by sacred testimony—
There is a right turn,
A struggle through purgatories of many names,
A rising to one's real being
Wherein one finds oneself linked with
The real beings of other men, and in God;
The kingdom *exists*, and is to be *entered*.
This seeming detour meanwhile leads
To a near highway just beyond where all roads end,
And along this, despite the prowlers of this planet,
Men and women can love one another,
Find their plot, build their world,
Live this life with unstreaked dignity
And lift a rainbow to the heavens.

White meridian, white light,
Dynamic atom-aggregate,
Lay waking on an inland lake.

To depression
The stock of debris descends,
Down go its greed-events,
Control by fear, prejudice, and murder.
Let go!
What value this, paper of the past,
Engraved, ingrained, meaningless?
What life, that for words and figures,
For power to spend and rear vain monuments,
Two hold guns and the rest are destitute?
Let go—and we'll carry all America in our hearts.
This is no ship we want to sink with,
But wreckage;
This is no ark through deluge into the future,
But wreckage manned by homesick ghosts.
Let go!
Let it go that we may live.
A pin, a watch-fob, a card of identification,
A name, pain, and emptiness,
A will to perpetuate what has been, blind
To distinctions between the useful and the useless,
And, of course, an ego.
Let go!
That which you have held now holds you.
And as it sinks would drag you down.
A chair of pessimism, a desk of disillusion,
Doors and windows of despair,
Denials run wild, violence,
Rampant negatives—
A fine suite, it is said—
A modern office
Machined and ventilated
For everything but man.

Walk from it,
Wake from it,
From the terrible mistake
That we who have power are less than we should be.
Join that staff whose left hand is
Demolishing defectives,
Whose right is setting up a mill
And a wheel therein, its rim of power,
Its spokes of knowledge, its hub of conscience—
And in that same heart we will hold all life.
It is the world we live in
Then let us live in it.

Islanders, newly come upon the continents,
If to live against annihilation,
Must outgrow themselves and their old places,
Disintegrate tribal integrators,
And fix, as their center of gravity,
As their compelling ideal
The symbol of Universal Man—
Must outgrow clan and class, color,
Nationalism, creed, all the fetishes
Of the arrested and dismembered,
And find a larger truth in larger hearts,
Lest the continents shrink to islands,
Lest human destiny abort
And man, bristling against himself, explode.

So I, once an islander, proclaim,
Not as if I were the first,
But remembering one who went before me.

Our crocks are adequate and breathed upon,
Shaped first by hand, now machined,
But not whole. Cracks are in them,
Lids shut out the radiant air,
Shut in unholy rust,

And we, incontinent
Or small by shrinkage,
As if souls were denim,
Are tight after the wash of experience.
Yet we are not, nor are we made
Of cheap materials;
Throughout we are perpetuating stuff,
Existing in every world conceived by man,
Enduring in the real world itself,
Made to flow and expand
Through feasts and fasts,
Through sufferings and ecstasies
To balance, and the sacred reconciliation.

Mend and stretch, and then—

Unlock the races, Open this pod by outgrowing it,
Free men from this prison and this shrinkage,
Not from the reality itself
But from our prejudices and preferences
And the enslaving behavior caused by them,
Eliminate these—
I am, we are, simply of the human race.

Uncase the nations,
Open this pod by outgrowing it,
Keep the real but destroy the false;
We are of the human nation.

Uncase the regions—
Occidental, Oriental, North, South—
We are of Earth.

Free the sexes
From the penalties and proscriptions
That allegedly are laid on us
Because we are male and female.

Unlock the classes,
Emerge from these pockets;
I am, we are, simply of the human class.

Expand the fields, the specializations,
The limitations of occupation,
The definitions of what we are
That gain fractions and lose wholes—
I am of the field of being,
We are beings.

Open the religions, the exclusive creeds,
Those tight parodies of God's intention;
There is a Root Religion
And we are of it, whose force transforms,
Whose way progressively reveals
The shining terraces of one reality.

Uncase, unpod whatever blocks, until,
Having realized pure consciousness of being,
Knowing that we are beings
Co-existing with others in an inhabited universe,
We will be free to use rightly with reason
Our own and other human functions—
Free men, whole men, men connected
With one another and with Deity.

In another Wall Street of the world
The stock of value ascends.
What then am I bid,
By what free arm and yielding hand,
Offering what currency,
For this.—

Matrons of shrinkage,
Feed not on these children,
But rather break your arms

Than impede their growth;
Lift those shadows,
Cut the binds of apron-strings,
That young gods may dance.

The skins have dried, so let them pass,
So let those who once lived and garnered
Release all seeds to us,
That we in turn may plant and gather
And pass on to those to come
Sound grain, right soil, air, rain and sun.

The cold white eye is in cold storage,
Down is the ad that reads,
"A dime to heaven in an elevator,"
And in this sacred factory
Of minerals, plants, animals and man,
Right direction is in his hands—
Man, master of himself and husbandman
Of earth and growth and every breathing creature,
Thus to live, thus to work, thus to love.

It is a new America . . .
In brand new cities,
Slanting up incredible buildings,
Bright pilasters are pathways to the sun.

I held a fair position as men rate things,
Even enviable—
I could taste flavors in a grain of sand,
My eyes saw loveliness,
And I had learned to peal the wind,
In short, I was a lucky fellow.
People shook my hand, said nice things,
And sometimes slapped me on the back;
Curious, then, that I, of all people,
In the month of the nastiest mouth,

Should have found myself caught
In a backbay leased by public and private
    scavengers;
Such was the case—but I found
A river flowing flowing backward to its source.

I met a woman—
Much that I am I owe to her,
For she was going where I was going,
We together,
And a buried being was called to life,
A beauty and a power, a revelation
Of what life is for, and why we are;
Except that on the way we parted.
Why? Who knows what breaks the whole?
Ego? Separation occurred and each re-tasted
The illusion of split dominance.
I and she pushed we apart,
We divided us—
There was no use staying,
The essential thing had been lost
And we would have helped each other lose it more,
So off we went, and singly buried it.
She entered a world, all hers only;
It is for her to say if it is hers or not.
You can have the world I wound around me,
Though I would not wish it on an enemy.
Now and then I see her from a distance,
Sharply remember our way together,
And feel, deep beneath the layers,
Gratitude—and the task of man.

Upon my phonograph are many records
Played on sides in sacred and profane extremes;
Sometimes I hear Gregorian chants
Or Bach's "It Is Consummated";
Sometimes I hear Duke Ellington

Or Eddy Duchin sing popular contemporary;
And some rare times
I hear myself, the unrecorded,
Sing the flow of I,
The notes and language not of this experience,
Sing I am,
As the flow of I pauses,
Then passes through my water-wheel—
And those radiant others, the living real,
The people identical in being.
Water-wheel, as the unending stream flows
To turn thee to thy function,
Send thy power to the stones
That they may grind, that we may live,
And do it excellently,
But may thy motions sometimes pause,
May you be still within the flow
That always was and always is.

Sun upon clean water is the radiance of creation—
And once, far out in the vast spread,
Our eyes beheld a sacrament;
Her face was marvelously bright,
My brain was fiery with internal stars,
I felt certain I had brought
The gods to earth and men to heaven;
I blessed her, drawing with the fingers
Of my spirit the figure of the cross;
I said to her—
"All my senses will remember you as sweet,
Your essence is my wonder."

  Sweetheart of the lake!
  Marvel of the prairies with starry eyes!
  Angel child! Princess of earth!
  Girl of the mesas and the great red plains!

Star of the sky! Joy of the sun!
Pride of the eagle! Beloved of the thunderbird!

It is a new world,
A new America

Fifty times walk up the Palmolive Building,
Or the Empire State, following the pilasters,
And, if it is the Empire State, you will find
On top at last a curious mooring-mast,
If the Palmolive, a curious revolving light;
Above you will arch a strange universe,
Below you spread a strange earth,
Beside you will stand a strange man.

To be spiritualized by each new American

Curious engine, compact of gleaming steel,
Trees, bone, blood, and compressed steam,
Your cabin is the captain's house,
Your whistle is the eagle's scream,
Accelerate your driving-rods—
Irresistible the whirling drive of great wheels.
Thundering black fire-being, down straight-a-ways
You roar with demonic speed, leaving
In your wake evident world-rails;
The double accents of your rods proclaim,
"My captain has new fuel and direction,
He will thunder me past semaphores,
Through blocks of all dimensions,
Past waiting stations and waiting beings,
Past all determined symmetries,
Beyond my headlight's searching reach . . ."
Irresistible the whirling drive of great wheels.

Each new American—
To be taken as a golden grain
And lifted, as the wheat of our bodies,
To matter superbly human.

The old gods, led by an inverted Christ,
A shaved Moses, a blanched Lemur,
And a moulting dollar,
Withdrew into the distance and died,
Their dust and seed sifting down
To fertilize the seven regions of America.
This new God we have—
Man at last triumphant over not-man,
Being born above anti-being,
And in this being, and everywhere,
The god who is, the God we seek.

The old peoples—
The great European races sent wave after wave
That washed the forests, the earth's rich loam,
Grew towns with the seeds of giant cities,
Made roads, laid silver rails,
Factoried superb machines,
Died and came alive again
To demonstrate the worth of individuals,
The purpose of the commonwealth.

Blood does mix with the stuff upon our boards
As water with flour to make bread,
And we have yeast, and we have fire;
To implement ourselves by things,
To use as means, what we are, what we have
    become,
Americans, to suffer and rejoice, create,
To live in body and all births;
And we can eat, and we can breathe,
And we can move, and we can circulate,

And we can love and bear love's fruit
For we are men and women living.

The great African races sent a single wave
And singing riplets to sorrow in red fields,
Sing a swan song, to break rocks
And immortalize a hiding water boy.

Earth is earth, ground is ground,
All shining if loved.
Love does not brand as slave or peon
Any man, but feels his hands,
His touch upon his work,
And welcomes death that liberates
The poet, American among Americans,
Man at large among men.

The great red race was here.
In a land of flaming earth and torrent-rains,
Of red sea-plains and majestic mesas,
At sunset from a purple hill
The Gods came down;
They serpentined into pueblo,
And a white-robed priest
Danced with them five days and nights;
And pueblo, priest, and Shalakos
Sank into the sacred earth
To resurrect—
To project into this conscious world
An example of the organic;
To enact a mystery among facts—
The mime-priest in the market-place,
Daubed with mud to grace the fecund,
Clown, satirist, and invocator,
Free dancer—
In the Corn Dance, the Koshare.

A strong yes, a strong no,
With these we move and make drama,
Yet may say nothing of the goal.
Black is black, white is white,
East is east, west is west,
Is truth for the mind of contrasts;
But here the high way of the third,
The man of blue or purple,
Beyond the little tags and small marks,
Foretold by ancient seers who knew,
Not the place, not the name, not the time,
But the aim of life in men,
The resultant of yes and no
Struggling for birth through ages.

We are the new people,
Born of elevated rock and lifted branches,
Called Americans,
Not to mouth the label but to live the reality,
Not to stop anywhere, to respond to man,
To outgrow each wider limitation,
Growing towards the universal Human Being;
And we are the old people, witnesses
That behind us there extends
An unbroken chain of ancestors,
Ourselves linked with all who ever lived,
Joined with all future generations;
Of millions of fathers through as many years
We are the breathing receptacles.

There is greatness in the truth,
A dignity to satisfy our wish,
A solemn tone to make us still,
A sorrow to fill our hearts,
A beauty and a vision in the truth.

Mankind is a cross,
Joined as a cross irrevocably—
The solid stream sourcing in the remote past,
Ending in far off distant years,
Is the perpendicular;
The planetary wash of those now living
Forms the transverse bar—
This, our figure on this globe.
And upon our God we are a cross,
And upon ourselves we are a cross,
And through life and death
And all the currents, we are held to it.

O thou, Relentless Stream . . .

The Mississippi, sister of the Ganges,
Main artery of earth in the western world,
Is a sacred river
In the spirit of our people;
Whoever lifts the Mississippi
Lifts himself and all mankind,
Whoever lifts himself
Makes that great brown river smile;
The blood of earth and the blood of man
Course swifter and rejoice when we spiritualize.

The west coast is masculine,
The east coast is feminine,
The middle region is the child—
Reconciling force
And generator of symbols,
Source of a new force—

My life is given to have
Realized in our consciousness,
Actualized in life without celebrity,
This real: wisdom empowered: men growing

From womb to birth, from birth to rebirth,
Up arcs of brightness to the resplendent source.

No split spirit can divide,
No dead soul can undermine thee,
Thou, great coasts and harbors,
Mountains, lakes, and plains,
Thou art the majestic base
Of cathedral people;
America,
The seed which started thee has grown.

The prairie's sweep is flat infinity,
The city's rise is perpendicular to farthest star,
I stand where the two directions intersect,
In any town or county in the land,
Level with my fellow men,
Right-angled to the universe;
Where God's dimensions touch our lives
And work their nameless magic.

Blue Meridian, banded-light,
Dynamic atom-aggregate,
Awakes upon the earth;
In his left hand he holds elevated rock,
In his right hand he holds lifted branches,
He dances the dance of the Blue Meridian
And dervishes with the seven regions
of America, and all the world.

Lift, lift, thou waking forces!
Let us have the power of man,
The tender power of the loving hand,
The irresistible urge
Of brain and heart and limbs
Moving on and on
Through the terms of life on earth

And then beyond
To aid the operations of the cosmos.

   Beyond plants are animals,
   Beyond animals is man,
   Beyond man is God.

   The Big Light,
   Let the Big Light in!

O thou, Radiant Incorporeal,
The soul of our universe, hurl
Down these seaboards, across these continents,
The thousand-rayed discus of thy mind,
And above our waking limbs unfurl
Spirit-torsos of exquisite strength!

PEERS

A rock, you are called,
And hard to touch,
No eyes, no mouth,
Yet we are peers since
You exist and I exist.
Some day I will see again
Your substance in the sacred flame
And meet you undisguised
In the root of all that lives.

LIVING EARTH

Who says that the Earth is blind?
Who have not seen the tiger's eye
In an almost face,
Who have not met the thousand eyes
Within the voice,
And the one great eye of the belly.

What life force, what sculptor within the body,
What organ is unseeing save that we are
Phrased to call consciousness?
Is not Earth, Being,
Is it not a core of life,
Has it not organisms with spine,
Glands, entrails, and a sage navel?
Is it not a field of Force,
Force and field living?
"Blind" force? "Accident?"
The only accident is
To attribute to the universe the blindness
That is fixed in ourselves.
Of thee, Earth, I would ask
Is spirit bonded to your body
In make-believe,
Or is body related to spirit in the real?
This chiefly I would know,
This chiefly I would see,
To understand if men are like
The other full-equipped members of the cosmos
Or exceptions.

WORDS FOR A HYMN TO THE SUN

We, limbed beings of the Earth,
With speech, with sight in day, the brain
Of Nature and her highest voice—
Viced in suffering we rise
And for all creatures thank thee, Sun,
Source of our existences.

Thou art the resplendent mood,
The joyous face of all our days,
Who makest winter love summer,
Each ripe season beget the next—
The Earth is thine eternal bride,
And as venerating children

We, limbed beings of thy birth,
With speech, with sight in day, the brain
Of Nature and her highest voice—
Viced in suffering we rise
And for all creatures thank thee, Sun,
Source of our existences.

MEN

Different in persons
Diverse in minds
Friends in understanding

Exiles in self
Antagonists in egotism
Brothers in being

Enemies in greed
Dull in routine
Lovers in beauty

Separate in bodies
Many in desires
One in ultimate reality

Strangers on the earth
Prisoners in this world
Natives of deity

PEOPLE

To those fixed on white,
White is white,
To those fixed on black,
It is the same,
And red is red,
Yellow, yellow—
Surely there are such sights
In the many colored world,
Or in the mind.
The strange thing is that
These people never see themselves
Or you, or me.

Are they not in their minds?
Are we not in the world?
This is a curious blindness
For those that are color blind.
What odd passions,
What queer beliefs
That men who believe in sights
Disbelieve in seers.

O people, if you but used
Your other eyes
You would see beings.

The Indians beat drums, sing and dance to assert themselves as human beings (or to surrender themselves?) in the vast universe that comes to earth in New Mexico.

Perhaps, too, they have quiet rituals which swing the body-mind to acquiescence, that the faculties the outer world knows nothing of, may gain the wakefulness which relates a man to higher worlds.

When I leave places that men call great and return to the State of which I am curiously native, I beat thoughts against the drum of mind, sing music that never leaves my instruments, and dance without gestures to assert myself (or to surrender myself?) in the same universe that comes to the same earth.

There are some things so basic that they are seldom mentioned between men. Yet they come out now and again, and it is one of these I honestly inscribe upon that ether, the memory of earth, above the Rio Grande, from Taos and above Taos, to Santa Fe and below Santa Fe.

There is an Exile in me, and sometimes I am him, and when I am, the mountains of the Southwest, each cliff and peak, all ridges and even the flat lands arise from an ancient deluge that I may be engulfed again, or crushed, or driven out.

You there who have seen me but did not realize the Exile, who have seen this body of a man and a human mask walking plazas in Taos and Santa Fe and the main street of Española, how could you know my feeling that the earth and all her Nature, that heaven and all its gods were gunning for cosmic outlaws, you and I being of the driven band?

Adobe walls are friendly to the touch because hands put them there, but I recall times when I was my exile in New Mexico, when even within these walls, and friends around, and piñon burning in the fireplace, the walls exposed me to at-one-ment or extinction.

And there is a Being in me. Sometimes, though rarely, I am him, and when I am, there is such marvel in the Rio Grande, such ecstasy of inner sun to outer sun, or inner breath to the blazing winds, that I and everyone seem re-born upon that ark which still rides high, straight above the mesas of all sunken lands.

I remember one twilight I walked into Santa Fe, and you were walking with me, but did not know it—or did you? You, the beings of many people who have no names to distinguish you as on plazas. We moved together, descending as from a hill, yet ascending in spiral, and came upon the essence of piñon as it arose from the houses into an air so marvelous that even Being took it in and was enhanced.

So I know that the struggle of Being and Exile, the central contest which no man resolves until he gives utter allegiance to the radiant, can be won and celebrated by mended instruments, as that of us which belongs to it rises, and blends with the vast universe that comes to earth in New Mexico.

I SIT IN MY ROOM

I sit in my room.
The thick adobe walls
Are transparent to mountains,
The mountains move in;
I sit among mountains.

I, who am no more,
Having lost myself to let the world in,
This world of black and bronze mesas
Canyoned by rivers from the higher hills.
I am the hills,
I am the mountains and the dark trees thereon;
I am the storm,
I am this day and all revealed,
Blue without boundary,
Bright without limit
Selfless at this entrance to the universe.

ROLLING, ROLLING

Rolling, rolling,
Emily, Emily.

Rolling away to Santa Fe,
Over the golden rails,
From white buildings to adobes,
From boulevards to trails,
Rolling away to Santa Fe,
My darling Emily.

From the prairies to the mesas,
From the blue lake to red plains,
To the sacred mountain where the eagle sails,
Over the golden rails,
Rolling away to Santa Fe,
My darling Emily.

Rolling, rolling,
Emily, Emily.

IT IS EVERYWHERE

There's a life awaiting on a rocky coast
Where blue sea waters
Spray the land
And blow across a town
Of prim white houses with green shutters;
I've seen there memorials to captains—
I must be going
There's a life awaiting in New England.

There's a life awaiting on the seaboard,
In the key of states,
The Empire town,
And all along to that city
Of my birth,
Washed by the Potomac
Trapped by Meridian Hill;
Something slanted on this coast
To sweep westward
And encircle the globe;
And when I think of how
That seed has grown—
I must be going,
There's a life awaiting on the seaboard.

There's a life awaiting in the Blue Ridge,
By an old church with bullet holes;
And strolling south . . .
Red soil, cane, and cotton-fields,
White particles and black loam;
I've seen the swamps
And I've seen the flowering,
Heard songs—
I must be going,
There's a life awaiting in the South.

There's a life awaiting in the hills,
Northwest of the prairies
In a rolling land
Through which an old brown river flows;
When the geese come down
In the greatest v's you've ever seen,
Honking, flying high, swift and sure—
I must be going,
There's a life awaiting in the Northwest.

In the great grey plains
Of far reaches
By an inland sea and golden dunes,
And a fabulous arising city,
This the matrix of America,
The gathering, the giving out,
And when the sun shafts down
To intersect this blessed earth—
I must be going,
There's a life awaiting in the Middle-West.

There's a life awaiting in the land
Of flaming earth, canyons,
Stark mesas and red valleys,
Brown birth
The grandeur of this planet;
A giant hand holds pueblos
And adobes,
Swift limbs dance the marriage
Of the eagle and the thunderbird;
And as I dream—
I must be going,
There's a life awaiting in the Southwest.

There's a life awaiting on the Coast,
Land's end,
The in-turn of a nation and a new birth,

Where mountains
Shoulder to the ocean,
And men build paradise
Above earthquakes,
And what comes down goes up again
Within the view of purple hills,
Tropic foliage,
And the dream-factory of the world;
A beckoning—
I must be going,
There's a life awaiting in California.

THE CHRISTIAN

EXISTENTIAL PERIOD

(1940–1955)

VAGUE OPENING

It was perhaps no accident
That drove me smash against this earth
And caused friction just enough
To fuse me with the planet's dust
Which cannot leave this spatial sphere
And thus, obeying law, binds me.

It is as if there were one God
In the universe, who, at the moment
Of my birth, pinched my eyes to pin-points,
And made me go blind through years;
Who now, just now, has touched my sight
To some vague opening; who says,
"It is a matter of indifference to me
Whether you see more, or not."

Thou, the Very Highest, who
For loving me, didst spell oblivion
In dust, and therein breathe my name.

DESIRE

Through this suffering and the opened heart
I seek the universal love of beings;
May I be made one with that love
And extend to everything;
I turn towards that love,
In this new season of a forgotten life
I move towards the heart of love
   Of all that breathes;
I would enter that radiant center
   and from that center live.

NOT FOR ME

Not for me—and may nothing enhance
But all dissolve me—except for my
Surrender to Thy Self, do I ask
Thy sanction for this work;
But for that in man, the pivot,
The bender of forces, upon which depends
Transport from exile to deep being;
That as broken instrument
I may be mended, as an agent
To do Thy Will towards man,
And the awakening of kinsmen.

Of the thousand things mind could write,
Guide it to the essential, hold it,
Single and intent upon the essential.
Not for me, except for my surrender
To the One Self, do I ask Thy sanction
For this work; but for that in man
Upon which depends the transport
Of consciousness from exile
To the pure essence of life,
To the deep center of being,
That as agent I may do Thy Will
Towards man, and the awakening of kinsmen.

THE CHASE

I have seen a hawk chase white pigeons
In a wild tumultuous flight,
The birds flying for their life
High up, until lost in the sky,
And the sun caught them,
And they never came back.

As the white bird leaves the dirty nest,
Flashes in the dazzling sky,
And merges in the blue,
May my spirit quit me,
And fly the beam straight
Into thy power and thy glory.

CLOUD

I lay on the great shadow
Wondering
Who cast this livid cloud
Between
Living beings and the salient light.

MOTION AND REST

Intent and thrilled I have watched birds fly
      and come to rest.
So would I move. So would I come to rest.
I have watched white birds wing and glide
      between me and a blue sky.

I have watched white birds alight on
      a barn roof
And come to rest, instantly still,
      effortlessly relaxed and poised,
In them no trace of former motion.

So would I come to rest, so should we
Come to rest at quiet time.

OUR GROWING DAY

Awaken us to the long day of the spirit
To the sun more radiant than the eyes can see;
Bring us low, if we are falsely raised
    in conceit
Bathe us in bright humility
Sweeten us, if we are filled with bitterness
    and prejudice,
Plow us, if we are hard and encrusted,
Plow us deeply and make us ready to grow.

May the seeds of men, planted in the fertile
but dark earth, spring up and grow
    splendidly
Sending the issue of their growing upward
Towards the kingdom, and outward
    to their brothers.

MENDED

The double I,
The cleft sky,
The parted ocean,
The fissured land,
Healed over by the passing hand.

PRAYER (I)

How we have strained at our dark works;
Permit us to do thy work of light.

> Take us into thy reality,
> Blend us with thy being.

ONE WITHIN

Whose life connects
The migratory sea
The sky serene
The restless mind
The quiet being
The light that sees
The black that shines
The voice that speaks
The unutterable mystery

THE PROMISE

Spring has no promise more than frost
For us; it does not say that men
Will bud and burgeon in new birth,
The legions of the buried resurrect
To greet the Son, he come within,
The very season of his outward leaving;
It is not guaranteed that God,
Coming from the south with light and love,
Will touch the seed, melt our crusts
And bestir Himself in us
When earth moves from cold to warmth.

The promise not contained in earthly change
Is given in the nature of our long growth,
The cycles of the soul are sure as those
Of sap, the spirit breaking free at last;
Not death but resurrection is the end,
All being born will be born again
And men bestir themselves in God—
Not death to God but life in him—
Winter shall give way to spring within.

THEY ARE NOT MISSED

Old paths forget the bruised feet,
Ancestral trees their fallen leaves,
Old houses doze upon the sprees,
The births and deaths that echo in
Their rooms. No sorrow feels our God,
The ancient one, for souls who shared
His glory once, long ago.
They are not missed, but now must seek
Or sink and some ascend towards Him,
Till past and present meet, and time ends.

TO GURDJIEFF DYING

Thou Venerene ascending to desire,
Knowing the Buddhic law but to pervert
Its power of peace into dissevering fire,
Coiled as a serpent round the phallic Tau
And sacramental loaf, yet still alert
To turn the nether astral light athwart
The beam ethereal, wherefore now art thou
Snake and seducer, Son of the Elder Liar?

Thou hast deformed the birth-bringings of light
Into lust-brats of black imaginings,
Spilling Pan-passions in the incarnate round
Of hell and earth. Lords of the Shining Rings
Skilled in white magic, may your skills abound!
Save even Gurdjieff from his hell forthright.

SEE THE HEART

Those who have ceased to love
Have not ceased to need,
Those who have ceased to care
Have not ceased to bleed;
Do not weigh the words that
Never ask, the minds that never
Seek, nor mark the averted faces,
   But see the heart.

A PUBLICATION HISTORY OF

THE POETRY OF JEAN TOOMER

THE AESTHETIC PERIOD (1919–1921)

"Five Vignettes" was first published in *Black American Literature: Poetry*, ed. Darwin Turner (Columbus, Ohio: Charles E. Merrill, 1969).

"Storm Ending" first appeared in *Double Dealer* 4, no. 21 (September 1922): 146. This poem, "Her Lips Are Copper Wire," "Evening Song," and "Face" are included in the Aesthetic Consciousness rather than the Ancestral Consciousness period on the basis of topical references in correspondence between Waldo Frank and Jean Toomer.

"And Pass" was first published in *The Wayward and the Seeking*, ed. Darwin Turner (Washington, D.C.: Howard University Press, 1980).

"Her Lips Are Copper Wire" first appeared in *S4N* 26 (May 1923).

"I See Her Lovely There" is published here for the first time. Toomer's unpublished poems comprise a large part of the Jean Toomer Collection, which from 1962 until 1985 was located at Fisk University, Nashville, Tenn. In December 1985, the Toomer Collection was moved to the Beinecke Rare Book and Manuscript Library at Yale University, New Haven, Conn.

"Evening Song" first appeared in *Cane* (New York: Boni and Liveright, 1923).

"Face" first appeared in *Cane*, p. 8.

"Air," "Earth," "Fire," and "Water" (formerly unpublished). In his handwritten notes for these lyrical sketches, Toomer hints at the symbology behind his linguistic impressionism: "Variety—air, fire"; "fire will carry out the spirit, earth—the letter"; "Intention [or] Plan—fire, earth. Air and water tend to leave to chance." In terms of time, he associates earth with the past, air with the present, and water with the future. Moreover, the poet associates air and fire with restlessness and activity, whereas water is "passive" and the earth is "resistant" and "conservative." He images sensuousness as the commingling of earth and fire. These notes are located in the Jean Toomer Collection, Box 50 Folder 63.

"Poem in C" (formerly unpublished).

"Sound Poem" (I) and "Sound Poem" (II) (formerly unpublished).

"Skyline" (formerly unpublished) is one of the few poems by Toomer with an urban setting.

"Gum," which also depicts an urban setting, first appeared in *Chapbook* 36 (April 1923): 22.

"Delivered at the Knighting of Lord Durgling" (formerly unpublished).

Reminiscent in style, imagery, and voice of Robert Frost, "Banking Coal" was first published in *Crisis* 24, no. 2 (June 1922): 65.

THE ANCESTRAL CONSCIOUSNESS PERIOD (1921–1923)

"Reapers," "Cotton Song," "Nullo," "Conversion," "Portrait in Georgia," "Beehive," and "Prayer" were first published in *Cane*. "November Cotton Flower" first appeared in *Nomad* (1923); "Song of the Son" in *Crisis* 23, no. 6 (1922): 261; "Georgia Dusk" in *Liberator* 5, no. 9 (September 1922): 25; and "Harvest Song" in *Double Dealer* 4, no. 24 (December 1922): 258.

The facsimile copy of "Tell Me" (formerly unpublished) bears the postscript "July 1922. Harpers Ferry: Washington."

THE OBJECTIVE CONSCIOUSNESS PERIOD (1924–1939)

Composed in Yeatsian imagery and revelatory of Toomer's own quest for unity of being, "The Lost Dancer" was first published in *Black American Literature: Poetry*, ed. Turner.

"Honey of Being" was first published in *The Wayward and the Seeking*, ed. Turner. Toomer completed two other versions of this poem, the first, called "Home":

> Always your heart, atomic symbol,
> Wherein experience returns
> To essence and reveals source
> And end identical; your love,
> Beauty and intelligence—
> Our aspirations seek, and,
> Having found, in ecstasy
> Fold their wings upon fulfillment.

and the second, "Home of Being":

> Always your heart, atomic symbol,
> Wherein experience returns
> To essence and I know source
> And end identical; your love,
> Reason and creativeness
> Our aspirations seek, and,
> Having found, in ecstasy
> Fold their wings upon fulfillment.

"Honey of Being" is apparently the final version.

"Angelic Eve" first appeared in *The Wayward and the Seeking*, ed. Turner.

"Merl" (formerly unpublished).

"White Arrow" first appeared in the *Dial* 86 (July 1929): 596. Like "Angelic Eve," it employs images of waking and sleeping drawn from Gurdjieffian philosophy.

"Unsuspecting" (formerly unpublished).

"The Gods Are Here" (formerly unpublished).

"At Sea" first appeared in *Black American Literature: Poetry*, ed. Turner. This poem images a mystical experience, as in "The Gods Are Here."

"Upward Is This Actuality" (formerly unpublished) bears the postscript "Jean Toomer. The Dunes. June 19 27."

"As the Eagle Soars" was first published in *Crisis* 41, no. 4 (April 1932): 116.

"Be with Me" (formerly unpublished) appears in neither Toomer's 1931 nor his 1934 projected volumes of verse. It does appear in his later projected volume "The Wayward and the Seeking" (ca. 1940). This suggests that the poem was probably written between 1934 and 1940. In its interpretation of what is ostensibly ancestral consciousness, the poem is curiously haunting.

A variation of the first 125 lines of "The Blue Meridian" was first published as "Brown River, Smile" in *Pagany* 3 (Winter 1932): 29–33. ("The First American," the germinal text for "Brown River, Smile," is not among Toomer's unpublished manuscripts and is apparently nonextant.) Several years later, a revised and expanded version of this text appeared in *New Caravan*, ed. Alfred Kreymborg, Lewis Mumford, and Paul Rosenfeld (New York: W. W. Norton and Company, 1936): 633–53 as "Blue Meridian" (no definite article). A revised version of the 1936 text appeared in *The Poetry of the Negro, 1746–1970*, ed. Langston Hughes and Arna Bontemps (Garden City, N.Y.: Doubleday, 1970): pp. 107–33. Darwin Turner adopts the 1970 text for inclusion in *The Wayward and the Seeking*, asserting that this latest draft constitutes Toomer's final version of the poem. I agree with Turner's assertion and have similarly adopted the 1970 text for inclusion in this volume.

"Peers" was first published in *The Wayward and the Seeking*, ed. Turner.

"Living Earth" (formerly unpublished) is a variant version of the poem "The Earth and Us." In accordance with his Ray of Creation theory, Gurdjieff maintained that the universe was "a living thing" and still growing.

"Words for a Hymn to the Sun" (formerly unpublished) is a tribute to Gurdjieff's Ray of Creation.

"Men" first appeared in *The Wayward and the Seeking*, ed. Turner.

"People" (formerly unpublished).

"Imprint for Rio Grande" was first published in *New Mexico Sentinel* on 12 January 1938. As in "I Sit in My Room," this poem was inspired by Toomer's love for the landscape and culture of the American Southwest.

"I Sit in My Room" (formerly unpublished).

"Rolling, Rolling" (formerly unpublished). Toomer wrote two other poems addressed to Emily, "Lucent Shield" and "Only Emily."

"It Is Everywhere" (formerly unpublished).

THE CHRISTIAN EXISTENTIAL PERIOD (1940–1955)

Although "Vague Opening" (formerly unpublished) appeared in Toomer's 1931 projected volume of poems, placing it in the Objective Consciousness period, this poem serves as an appropriate expression of religious consciousness as a corollary of Gurdjieffian idealism, as well as an appropriate link between Toomer's Objective Consciousness and Christian Existential periods.

There are three variant texts of "Desire": "For Unity," dated 6 March 1939; "For Conscience," dated 8 March 1939; and "For Union," dated 15 March 1939. All four poems are published here for the first time.

FOR UNITY
I, now locating in the outer man,
Seek the unifying principle in the
    inner being.
So shall I be drawn to unity,
So shall inner and outer become
    reciprocal and integrated,
and I attain normal human being.
I turn towards that will,
I feel towards the will of the
    unifying principle.

I would center that center,
and from that center live.

FOR CONSCIENCE
I, now locating in the outer man,
Seek the conscience in the inner being.
So shall I be drawn to being—responsibility
   in the cosmos,
So shall inner and outer become reciprocal and integrated
and I attain the norm of human being.
I turn towards that burning light,
I feel towards the will of the
   cosmic conscience.
I would center that center,
And from that center live.

FOR UNION
Like draws like.
May there be some inner man
   in the outer man;
So shall inner draw outer.
May there be some outer man
   in the inner man;
So shall outer draw inner.
So the two become as one,
   reciprocal and whole.
Otherwise each will go his way,
And unlike repel unlike,
The divided become more divided,
The man more split,
Until it is all but impossible
   for the two to meet.

Most of the imagery in these three latter poems is an expression of
Objective Consciousness, whereas in "Desire," which, although
undated is ostensibly the synthesis and final version of these poems,
the addition of the line "In this new season of a forgotten life"

suggests a change in perspective. Indeed, the images which comprise the closing lines reflect a shifted emphasis away from agape, or brotherly love, toward Logos, or God's love. The image of the self merging with "that radiant center" which is the heart of love, recalls the "Inner Light" of Quaker religious faith.

The facsimile copy of "Not for Me" (formerly unpublished) is dated "June 1, 1938." This poem is a variation of "Prayer for Mending."

The religious image of white birds in "The Chase" (formerly unpublished) also appears in "Motion and Rest."

"Cloud" (formerly unpublished) is a variation of the Japanese five-line tanka.

"Motion and Rest" (formerly unpublished) is a tranquil portrait of asceticism.

"Our Growing Day" (formerly unpublished) curiously employs a Gurdjieffian image of "awakening."

"Mended" first appeared in *The Wayward and the Seeking*, ed. Turner. Like "Cloud," this poem is a variation of the Japanese five-line tanka.

"Prayer (I)" (formerly unpublished).

"One Within" first appeared in *The Wayward and the Seeking*, ed. Turner.

"The Promise" (formerly unpublished) manifests the poet's acceptance of the paradox of religious faith in contrasting images of spring in nature and "new birth" in man.

In "They Are Not Missed" (formerly unpublished) the poet images God, time, and eternity in terms of Old Testament religious faith.

"To Gurdjieff Dying" (formerly unpublished).

"See the Heart" was first published in the Quaker journal, *Friends Intelligencer* 104 (9 August 1947): 423.